Indigo Child
and the
Spirit World

Indigo Child
and the
Spirit World

MARCEL LAPORTE

ARPress
ILLUMINATING IDEAS
EMPOWERING VOICES

ARPress
45 Dan Road Suite 5
Canton MA 02021

Hotline: 1(888) 821-0229
Fax: 1(508) 545-7580

Ordering Information:

Quantity sales. Special discounts are available on quantity purchases by corporations, associations, and others. For details, contact the publisher at the address above.

Printed in the United States of America.

ISBN-13:   Softcover   979-8-89330-719-1
                eBook   979-8-89330-720-7

Library of Congress Control Number: 2024901852

Foreword

We all know that life is a journey. We all take different paths in life and we try to do our best everyday. As we go forward, we often wonder why life is so complicated and try to understand why people say everything happens for a reason. As we search for answers, we might stumble upon things, or events that we cannot understand. We live in a world filled with events that we cannot avoid and some that we bring upon ourselves. There are worlds that we cannot see. This book makes reference to our world and the spirit world. Some of us are born with a sixth sense. We deal with both worlds on a daily basis. Some choose to believe, some not to believe. We need to get up and smell the coffee Satan does exist. There is an ongoing tug-of-war between god and the dark side. Have you ever wondered the reason why when someone is about to die and recites a prayer that includes the word? As I walk into the shadow of death, I will fear no evil. Take a moment to think about the meaning of that sentence.

Indigo Children

According to a pseudoscientific new age concept, these are children who believe to possess special, unusual, and sometimes supernatural traits and abilities.

Descriptions of an Indigo Child

- The belief that they are empathetic, curious, strong-willed, independent, and often perceived by friends as being strange.

- Possess a clear sense of self-definition and purpose,

- Exhibits a strong, innate subconscious spirituality from early childhood (which however, does not necessarily imply a direct interest in spiritual or religious areas)

- A strong feeling of entitlement , or deserving to be here.

- A high intelligence quotient, an inherent intuitive ability.

- A true indigo travels between worlds at night when we think they're sleeping.

- Indigos have an inner knowing that exceeds our psychic abilities.

- They are the next stage in human evolution , in some cases possessing paranormal abilities such as telepathy.

You can find more information on www.indigo.children.com

CONTENTS

Chapter 1

Growing up in a small town, the type that everyone knows everyone. You are subject to hear a lot of gossip, stories, rumors and events. A few words can start an avalanche of gossip that will be blown out of proportion.

Town folks compare details: E.g.: *Well I heard....And I know for a fact.....It comes from a reliable source....Heard it from the horse's mouth.* Strange no horses in town and can a horse talk?

At seventeen, you can be cocky and mister indestructible and smarter than your friends that's what I thought. If something is going to happen, it's not going to happen to me. I am smart enough to avoid any type of problems and by a small chance if I do get into a certain situation, I will be able to remedy the issue in a blink of an eye.

My friends were no different than the town's folks, they would tell me outrageous stories and I'd say, I need to see, to believe such nonsense. I would ask who told you that the town drunk, one of my friends replied.

"Come on, you know that I would not waste my time listening to him. He never makes any sense; he is always drunk. Anyway, last night, my neighbor gave my mom all the details."

"What details?"

"You know, about Mr. and Mrs. Blake."

"That story does not make any sense."

That's why, I never paid any attention to any of the rumors going around town especially when it comes to paranormal and religion.

I would say to my friends.

"Why talk about that nonsense on such a beautiful day. Do you guys want to be sorcerers, wizards or warlocks? Good luck guys on finding a school that you can go and learn all that stuff, which I believe is all fantasy. Did you guys cook a batch of nonsense in your black pots?"

In religion, Adam and Eve were white, there are so many different cultures of people living on this earth. Priests are being arrested for child abuse and pornography. As they say, the more science advances the more they are proving the bible wrong.

Growing up, my mom wanted me to go to church every Sunday. The pool hall was only three doors down the road. I would go into the church to pick up a church bulletin and out the door to go play pool. When I noticed the church goers exiting the church, I would inquire from someone the details of the priest's sermon and make my way home.

A blabbermouth squealed on me, so no more pool hall for me. So, every Sunday morning, my mom made sure that I did go to church. A spy would confirm to my mom that I went to church. For me it was a waste of time.

The author who wrote the bible; where did he get the facts? -- On television ministries keep asking for money. There is so much turmoil in this world. In high school, I did not care about religion classes. I was a rebel.

Rumors were circulating in town that a couple owned a flying cat. One night, my dad and I decided to go see if the rumors of a flying cat where true. I guess a lot of people had the same idea.

There was a long line -up of folks like us that wanted to see the flying cat. The ones that were fortunate to reach the cage were talking among themselves; about the way the cat was positioned in his cage and they could not tell if the cat had wings.

A man said to the owners,

"I waited in line for over an hour to see the cat. Let the cat out of the cage so that everybody will be able to see the cat fly."

The owners refused by saying they were afraid the cat would fly away and not come back.

"Sure, sure a good excuse."

We waited for a little while longer to see the famous flying cat. We went home with no proof of a flying cat. There you go, another one of many false rumors. Almost every day a new rumor would pop up. I guess it must be the same in every little town.

There was also rumors that every night, werewolves were roaming the streets. They do not have to wait for a full moon to transform into werewolves.

Apparently a lady had a chat with a man and when he walked away and turned the corner, she heard a wolf howling. She went to take a look and saw a wolf in the middle of the street. No trace of the man that she had a conversation with.

One rumor that was true is bats with rabies, which I did see. The rumor is, there were too many sinners in town and god sent the bats to punish them. Really? God would send bats to punish the sinners? I don't think so. One night, my friend's sister was walking home and was attacked by a bat.

She was able to fight him off and kill the bat by crushing him with her shoe. She rushed home, her dad retrieved the dead bat to get it analyzed for rabies. The test came back positive for rabies. As a precaution, my friend's sister was given a couple of needles around her belly button.

The town took action to get rid of the bats. Funny part is, there are still sinners in town but no more bats with rabies!

Another story was, if any children were outside after nine o'clock, the boogeyman would grab the children and take them away to never be seen again.

I watched television shows based on true events and laugh. I did not believe unseen entities could control your mind and make you hear voices.

My mom's sisters would come over and talk about spirits and demons. One of the stories was that a mother could hear her boy cry in his bedroom. She went to see the reason why he was crying and when she opened the door, the devil was spanking her son. Apparently, the boy was misbehaving. The mom warned her son that the devil would come and spank him.

Another story was that a teenage girl dared the devil to come and cut her hair. The story is that she woke up in the middle of the night and the devil was cutting her hair.

My response was, "Sure, Mom, if that's the case". She did get a free haircut. I said if the devil is real, I would like to see him try something like that with me. He would not stand a chance. My mom would say; be careful what you wish, for someone might be listening. I would say 'Yes, Mom', with a smirk on my face. She would say, "Don't do that! You might get a surprise visit".

I would say, "Look Mom, I am scared". She would warn me to not mock what I cannot see. I told her that I do not want to hear any more nonsense. I will never believe in that kind of stuff… but that was about to change.

Chapter 2

It was a nice sunny day, I remember telling my friends that it's hot for the month of June. I and seven of my friends were on our way home after writing our final exam to end the school year. We were all in a good mood goofing around, telling jokes. One of my friends suggested we should go swimming before going home. We all agreed that it was a great idea.

The river was not far from where we were. We went across a small field down a hill to reach the river bank. We stripped to our underwear; maybe that's one of the reasons moms would always say, make sure to have clean underwear.

We all jumped in the water. The water was a bit cold but refreshing. While swimming, one of my friends found an old raft on shore. It was made of old wooden poles and an old rope. It was large enough to hold all of us.

I was standing in the middle of the raft when it broke right down the middle. I was the first one in the water, everyone fell on top of me, pushing me down deeper under the water. I tried to resurface but was unable to do so, since their feet and legs are in the way. One of my friends accidentally hit me on the forehead with his heels and the hit really rung my bell. My friends were all trying to resurface themselves.

I started going down in the cold and darkness of the river. My ears and lungs started to hurt. I swallowed water, I could not breathe, there was water in my lungs. I was drowning. I felt a pair of hands trying to pull me up to the surface. My friend was able to get my head out of the water for a few seconds. My friend could not hold me as I was way too heavy, so I was going under again.

He was the smallest one in the gang and me being the biggest one in the bunch. I was way too heavy for him. He yelled for help and I passed out. I could not muster any energy to try and save myself from drowning.

My friends dove back in the water. They were able to bring me to the shore, but I was unresponsive. My friends were trying to revive me when a man came running to help; he was able to resuscitate me. The man was one of the city's employees, fixing a pump in the pumphouse that provides water for the town. He heard the commotion and came running to help.

Thank god, he knew CPR. When I opened my eyes, my friends were cheering and I saw the ambulance arriving. Man, what a headache, sore ears and sore throat! I remember I was cold and shivering. The first responders covered me with a blanket and whisked me away to the hospital. When the ambulance arrived at the hospital, my mom was already at the hospital with a worried look on her face.

She looked at me but did not say anything. When she got the word that I will be alright, she went home. I was breathing with help of an oxygen mask. She waved at me and she was on her way home. They kept me overnight for observation, and in the morning, I went home.

My dad was waiting for me in the car. On our way home, my dad mentioned that my mother was really upset with me. As soon as I got out of the car, I could see she was upset and relieved at the same time.

She asked me a bunch of questions. She wanted details on what happened. I made sure to answer all of her questions. When the question period was over, I had this to say,

"The things that people say about a near death experience about seeing a light, or dead relatives and feeling at peace; I am going to say it again-- it's all nonsense! All I remember is waking up spitting, vomiting, my friends were around me cheering and the ambulance arrived."

"I was worried sick until they brought you in the emergency room."

"So anyway, as I was saying, the experience justified my beliefs. When you kick the bucket, there is nothing but darkness. One question Mom, how did you get to the hospital so fast?"

"I was already at the hospital visiting your Aunt Sandra, when I heard the emergency ward preparing to receive a young patient that almost drowned. They mentioned your name, so I rushed to the emergency ward, that is why I was there when you arrived."

When you are trying to cope with an incident that you lived or witnessed, and no matter how you try to shake it off, it will not go away. It is embedded in your brain and it will simply not go away. When people say, 'it's over', 'it's in the past, get over it', is easier said than done. I always reply with a few choice of words. Also, they do not know what they are talking about.

Even today if I go up to my neck in the water, I start to struggle to catch my breath. I need to get out of the water as soon as possible. Before the incident, I could swim like a fish. Another thing, I will not tolerate any playing in a boat and if the goofing around continues, I bring the individuals back to shore. Some events stay with you for the rest of your life. So back to the story…

I reiterated to my mom, proof that all the stories she believes are all make believe.

"Look, Mom. In the bible, it is written that Adam and Eve were white and guilty of the first sin on this earth by taking a bite out of the apple given to them by the snake. Look at all the colored people with different religions and different gods."

"I know, but that's not the point."

"There's no point to be made mom. I personally think when they say that people are possessed by the devil, they suffer from what you call the bipolar disease or simply want attention. The nonsense about chain letters."

I kept on repeating if there are ghost and goblins out there. I want proof. I will be getting my proof in a very short while.

I still remember as if it was yesterday, when I went to bed that Monday night. I had an uneasy feeling. I shook it off as being tired. It only took me a few minutes before I fell asleep. Our house was located on a street corner with a four- way stop.

When the house was built, it included a basement, three bedrooms and, of course, a bathroom, living room, dining room, and a kitchen. The bedrooms where facing the back yard. The kitchen, dining room and living room where all facing the street.

With the addition of two brothers in the family, changes needed to be done. Thus, the living room was converted to a bedroom and the dining room into a living room. Now, my new bedroom was facing the street corner.

There were no curtains in the window, only a very thin white sheer. So at night, with the street light facing my bedroom window with only the sheer covering the window, I could navigate in my room without any problem even without the use of a light.

From my bed, I could easily see if someone entered my room. That fateful night, I was sound asleep with my back facing my bedroom door. Something woke me up and I could feel a presence in the doorway of my bedroom.

Still half asleep, I turned around to take a look. In the doorway, I could see a black mass that was almost like a shape of a man with red eyes and floating about four inches from the floor.

I said, I must be dreaming, and turned around again to go back to sleep with my back again facing the door. After a few seconds, I could feel a presence getting closer so again, I turned around and there it was, right beside my bed and leaning towards me!

I jumped out of bed and started running towards my parent's bedroom. I ran through the living room, the kitchen to get to the hallway. My parent's bedroom was at the end of the hallway, so I had to run to the end of the hallway to reach their bedroom.

It was a couple of inches from me breathing down my neck and when I burst into my parent's bedroom, it disappeared. My mom jumped out of bed and asked me what was wrong.

"You're pale as a ghost and shaking like a leaf, what is the matter?"

"I woke up and a black mass was looking at me and approaching my bed. The black mass followed me until I reached your door."

My mom replied with a little smile on her face.

"Maybe it was an alien seeing that you do not believe in the supernatural."

"Mom, it's not a time for jokes."

By now my dad was also awake.

"Go back to bed it was only a nightmare. You should be ashamed running to Mommy because you had a bad dream. You are seventeen years old for crying out loud, man up or else you will be a scary cat for the rest of your life. Do you understand?"

"Dad."

"Don't dad me. I heard you say many times nothing scares you so why are you in our bedroom.? Please go back to your room so that we can get some sleep. Thank you and goodnight."

My mom followed me to my room.

"I believe you. How many times did I warn you about your attitude and sarcastic comments about the paranormal?"

"Yes I know, but ..."

"You challenged them to come and see you, someone or something decided to take you up on your offer and decided to pay you a visit. Are you okay? Can I go back to bed? I have to get up in a few hours to go to work."

I told her I was fine. My mom went back to bed. I sat on the couch until morning.

Chapter 3

A few days went by with no further incidents.

"Mom, although I did not see anything since my near death experience, I felt that I was being watched all the time."

"Now that you witnessed what can happen when you are cocky and talk too much. There is a saying if you spit in the air too many times there is a chance that it might come back and hit you in the face, we warned you."

"I know Mom and I am sorry for my sarcasm but you know as well as I do, a rumor or a story can only have ten words in the morning and in the evening you could write a book."

"I know but decipher the common sense."

When my mom told my aunts about my encounter, they had a field day with me. My sisters made fun of me, they told my friends about me running to my mom to wake her up because I was scared.

I kept on telling them that I was not scared but confused. Sure, they would say with a big grin on their face, "you were confused now we understand why you ran to mommy you were confused makes a lot of sense." I had to endure cat calls, wisecracks all summer long.

My final year of high school, let's just say it was not very pleasant as if every student in the school except for a few friends banded together to really let me have it. Everyday, all I hear is"Mommy help me, I am scared" and all the nonsense that came with it.

I tried to keep my cool but on a few occasions, the teasing ended up in fisticuffs. They changed their attitude towards me when word got out that I was fighting back and I was good at it. I was not taking anymore shit from anyone.

My near-death experience opened a door that was kept shut, a brand new world that I did not know existed and certainly not prepared to deal with.

Wow, I will need to learn how to cope as I go along because at that point , I did not know what was happening and certainly no idea what the future would bring. I was baffled, confused, so many questions. Like they say, it will be on the job training.

My mom did not have all the answers. I became a very nervous young man to say the least, my head was spinning out of control so my mom told me.

"Relax and take life one day at a time. Try not to look too far in the future and assume what will happen or else you will go crazy."

"Mom, I think I am already halfway there."

"One day at a time, we cannot change yesterday, we can deal with today, because we do not know what tomorrow will bring. I am going to tell you something that only a handful of people know. My mom, your grandmother was known to be a witch."

"Really? Wow."

"Yes, but she was a good witch."

"I did not know there was such a thing as a good witch; to my knowledge, all the witches were bad."

"Not all of them. Everyday, people would go see her to do all sorts of tricks that did not make any sense, she also had to deal with ignorant bad people that's why she took life one day at a time."

"Makes sense."

"If I tell you a story today, will you believe me?"

"I guess so."

"We will see."

My mom told me when her grandfather died, he was working on a new set of sleighs. At night they could hear him in the shed working, hammering away to finish the job.

"Really, hammering away."

"When your grandfather- my dad retired at the age of sixty eight, he was struggling to make ends meet. He borrowed money from me. One night while watching television, he suffered a massive heart attack and died. Along with your grandmother, two of my sisters were still living at home."

"Yes, I remember that awful night."

"For about a month after my dad passed away, my mom would hear the kitchen cupboard doors open and close, she would also hear footsteps coming up the stairs."

"Really poor man."

"The steps paused for a moment in front of your Aunt's bedroom door and then the footsteps would continue and stop at your grandmother's bedroom door."

"For real?"

"He was checking up on them to see if everything was okay. He would do the same ritual every night until your grandmother told him."

"Wait a minute, grandmother made contact with him."

"Yes she did and said everything is good, we are okay. I appreciate your visits but it's time for you to go rest in peace and someday we will be reunited in heaven, get some well-deserved rest, I will see you when I get there."

One night, my grandfather came to see me in my bedroom. He was in the middle of a bright light. I could tell he was at peace and he let me know that he was going to comeback. I was his first and favorite grandson. When I told my mom, she was intrigued .

"He told you he would come back. Nothing else?"

"No, Mom. Nothing else."

"I wonder why he told you that?"

"I have no idea, Mom but let me tell you it was quite the surprise."

"I bet."

"I will let you know if he does come back?"

"Yes. Please."

That was the only time that my grandfather paid me a visit. Every Monday night or Tuesday morning, 1:20 A.M the exact time that I woke up that night and came face to face with the red-eyes black entity.

I would wake up, feel a presence in my room but could not see who or what it was. Whatever it was, it made sure that it could not be seen. He or she was probably sent by the black entity to agonize me.

I kept asking to show himself or talk to me. Every time that I would ask a question, it would go away. I even gave him or her a name, the invisible goblin. My mom suggested that I put a crucifix on my bed's headboard.

"What a great idea, I am going to get one today. Thanks, Mom."

"You're welcome! That's why we are moms to come up with great ideas to help."

That night before going to bed, I put a crucifix on the headboard of my bed. It worked no more visits from the invisible goblin. Finally, I was able to get a good night sleep.

There was also another annoying distraction that I had to deal with . My bedroom walls were covered with sheets of wooden veneer, very popular stuff at the time with different patterns.

Embedded in the wood, one of the patterns that was on the right beside my bed, when in bed and facing the wall, I could see the devil's ugly face staring at me. I asked both my sisters when looking at the patterns, "What do you both see?"

They replied,

"The face of a clown."

"Really the face of a clown?"

"Yes. If there is a devil's face in that pattern, we do not see it."

Every morning first thing , I would see was the devil's face. I moved my bedroom furniture around so that my bed faced another wall, no matter what I did, the face was always staring at me.

I covered my walls with posters. Everyday I would find at least one poster on the floor and that ugly face was always keeping an eye on me. I asked a few of my friends to look at the wall and to tell me what they saw.

They all said the same thing. A clown's face. It did not matter where I would point for them to look, same answer a clown's face.

My parents did not like the size of the living room it was too small, so they decided to move my bedroom in the basement so they could enjoy a larger living room.

My new bedroom walls were covered with drywall, no more ugly face to look at in the morning. When a few of my friends were in my new bedroom.

"Do you still see the devil's face on the wall?"

"No."

One of my friends replied.

"If it was the devil that was looking at you he would have found a way to keep annoying you don't you think?"

Another one of my friends replied,

"You want my opinion?"

"No."

"No but I will tell you anyway. It was your imagination, you were the only one that was able to see the face, are you going crazy on us?"

My friends were looking at me with a smile, another one of my friends also put in his five cents.

"You still get frustrated when we talk about it."

"To answer your question, I am already crazy to have friends like you guys. I do not appreciate your dumb comments, you guys are one step away from getting your ass kicked out of my house."

"Come on now, no reason to get so uptight."

"Although you guys do not believe or see what I see, that does not mean that I am crazy. It's enough I do not want to hear another word, you guys call yourselves my friends."

They apologized for teasing me. We went on with our day without anymore sarcastic remarks aimed at me.

After my swimming incident, I was always hearing whispers and see spirits. I did not know what to make of it. I started to get hunches or premonitions or predictions.

I had no clue how or why it was happening. I also noticed that I was always *Johnny on the spot* to help people in distress. I shook it off as coincidences.

I did not know what to do or what to say with everything that was happening. My mom advised me to go talk to a priest. I called our parish priest, made an appointment for the following afternoon.

The next day on my way to go see the priest, I ran into another one of my friends. We talked a little about life in general.

"Are you still being teased about your encounter?"

"No, I punched a few of those assholes in the face. Everything is quiet now."

"Good for you. Before I forget, do you remember a few months ago at Jason's party. The four girls playing with a ouija board, you know Karen, Julie and their two friends from the city."

"Yes, they were playing with the board in the living room, we all went in the kitchen. Nobody wanted to be in the same room with the girls while they were playing with the board. The girls called us chickens, whimps because we did not want to play the game."

"Guess what, I heard from a reliable source that Karen was involved in a car accident and suffered two broken legs, Julie's house burned to the ground and they lost everything."

"That's a shame. I feel for them but we did warn them when they were playing with the board that down the road it might cause them problems and look what happened. What about the other two girls, have they suffered any mishaps?"

"I don't know seeing that they are from out of town. I have no information or contact with either of them."

"Do you believe in the ouija board and other mysterious happenings?"

"I am starting to believe."

"You should believe. Remember when I was a non-believer, always making jokes about the whole thing, look what happened to me with my sarcastic comments. You know in the past I would dismiss situations as being coincidences; to me it was all nonsense, not anymore my friend."

"Yes I know but I am not going to poke my nose in that kind of stuff."

"I am on my way to see a priest in order to better understand what is going on, what to do with eveything that is happening to me. "

"Good luck, my friend. I hope the priest will be able to help you. See ya."

"Thanks, don't be a stranger."

"You as well. We will get together soon for a few cold ones."

"Yes, I would love that. Until next time, take care."

"I will and the same for you, my friend."

I continued to make my way to the priest's residence. When I got there, I hesitated for a few minutes, thinking is he going to believe me, listen to what I have to say.

I hope he can help me understand what the heck is going on with me. I finally decided to ring the doorbell. When he answered the door, his first words were.

"I was watching you from the window. I was not sure if you were going to ring the bell."

"Well, I am a little skeptical and shy at the same time to tell you what I have to say."

"Come on in, grab a seat. No need to be nervous and worry. What will be discussed in this room will stay in this room. I am here to listen and not pass judgement. You are not the first one to come see me and you won't be the last one either. Do you want something to drink?"

"A beer or some wine, I know you guys always have wine at hand."

He looked at me and smiled.

"Good you have a sense of humor. So, what can I do for you today?"

"Well, Father by now you must be aware of my swimming accident and I came close to meeting our maker. There would have been a funeral with me in the casket. Brrr scary thought."

"Yes. In a small town news or rumors spread like wildfire. Talk to me I am listening don't be shy tell me everything that you came here to discuss with me today, the more information that you provide will help me understand the reason for your visit today."

I proceeded by telling him what was happening. I was all over the place. I was nervous and eager to tell him everything.

"One step at a time, please. Like I said take your time or else we might be here all day. We can only deal with one issue at a time."

"Sorry about that. I guess I am overly anxious and afraid that I might forget important information that needs to be said for you to have a better picture of what I am talking about. Sorry, I will start over."

It took me about twenty minutes to explain the details of what was taking place and frustrating me because I was trying to make sense, understand, but I did not know what to do. He listened to what I had to say without disrupting me and make me lose my train of thought.

"You survived because it was not your time to go. You have not accomplished what you were sent to do. You have a lot of work ahead of you."

"What do you mean that I have a lot of work to do?"

"A lot is expected from you. Your near death experience opened doors that were kept shut because you were not a believer. Before that day, growing up did you have weird dreams that you were flying from one dimension to another, spirits paying you a visit?"

"Yes, almost every night but they were only dreams not reality. I was under the assumption that my dreaming of spirits was a way to manifest my disbelief of the supernatural, they were only dreams, not reality."

"Well let me be the first to tell you were not dreaming. Everything is real."

"I am totally confused about what you just said."

"I will explain in a minute, so by not believing in the paranormal you did not realize the importance of these events. It would have been a waste of a gift that was given to you by God."

"A gift by God"

"Yes, a gift from God. You would never be able to achieve your potential, your goal for being here. Something needed to be done, you must have heard the saying, God works in mysterious ways well."

"Can I interrupt you for a moment please? What I am hearing or your about to tell me that my brush with death was something that needed to be done in order for the famous doors to be opened.

Wow really? Could he have chosen a better way like send a message or something?"

"Would you have paid any attention to messages, signals?"

"I guess not, but how does it work that near death thing?"

"It's all part of your self conscious, what you kept shut or did not realize your reason to be here. Your brain does not control your thoughts anymore it's like your defense mechanism is shut off and releases some content in your brain that was never activated if you will."

"I have content of the paranormal in my brain."

"Yes, you do. Many individuals that go through near death experience, some become psychics, human angels, messengers, some are not so lucky it opens the door to the paranormal world, all that to say my friend it needed to be done in order for you to do your work. "

"It's crazy stuff. Are you sure about all of this?"

"Think about it, the city employee that was Johnny on the spot, your mom at the hospital visiting a relative. What are the odds for everything unfolding at the same time. Have you ever heard of Indigo children?"

"No."

"Well, what would you say if I told you that you are an Indigo child."

"You're basing your assumptions on what?"

"Look at all the evidence in front of you. I can see you are still confused."

"Yes, more now than ever."

The priest was very patient, he took the time to explain that it was perfectly normal to be confused. He also took the time to educate me what it meant to be me and what I will need to do.

"If I want to close the doors will I be able to do so?"

"Once opened they cannot be closed. I can see that you are still confused. What I can do is schedule a visit with an archbishop. They have a lot more knowledge than I do when it comes to indigo children. All right, anything else for today?"

"No, I don't think so."

"I will make some phone calls and get back to you."

"Thank you for your time and patience and all the information. I have to admit, I am still confused about certain things, don't get me wrong by saying that 'father you did clarify and answered a lot of questions'."

"Good."

"I am looking forward to meet the archbishop and see what he has to say so that I can fully understand and what to expect on a daily basis."

"I am glad that I was able to help. As soon as I have the time and date for you to see the archbishop, I will drop you a line."

"Thank you, father. Take care until next time."

"You too, I am certain that we will be talking again. Remember my door is always open."

"Great! One question… is the door to the wine cabinet always open?"

He started laughing.

"It won't be anymore."

"Will your door be open at two or three o'clock in the morning?"

"Go home you little smartass. Talk to you soon."

I went home with a better understanding and clarity but still confused for certain subjects that was discussed with the priest. When I got home, my mom was eager to know how the meeting went.

"It was very informative. I learned a lot but still confused for certain things. He suggested that I talk to a archbishop for me to better understand what is currently unfolding in front of my eyes and what the future holds for me. He told me that I was a indigo child. Mom have you ever heard of Indigo children?"

"Yes I have. We native-- you know first nation people; we are very spiritual and believe in the afterlife. Our elders that passed are still with us. I still cannot understand with your native background and not believe in the spirit world?"

"I was too stubborn and too much of a rebel to believe. Do you think by being native that it's one of the reasons that I am an indigo child?"

"Could be. The one that will maybe be able to answer that question is the archbishop."

It took a few days before I got the phone call that I was anxiously waiting for. When I hung up the phone, I told my mom that I would have to wait another week before meeting with the archbishop.

Chapter 4

The day finally arrived for me to visit the archbishop. I thought the day would never come, it was only a week but to me it was more like a month. That's how anxious I was.

I was feeling the same way when I went to see the priest; nervous and also afraid to tell him everything I needed to talk about.

All week I replayed in my head over and over what I wanted to talk about to be clear for him to understand my reasons to see him. His residence was about thirty minutes away.

Back in the day, it was easy to get your driver's license. You paid one dollar for a sixty days practice permit, read a book and you are ready for the written exam and driving test.

Which at that time, the test cost a whopping six dollars for both tests which are easy to pass so at the age of sixteen, I obtained my driver's license.

I borrowed my mom's car to go meet with the archbishop. When I arrived, the archbishop was outside sitting on a bench waiting for me.

When he stood up a big sigh of relief came over me. The archbishop was from my hometown, he was our parish priest for many years. We shook hands.

"By the look of surprise on your face, you were not aware it would be me that you were meeting today."

"No, Father Joseph only told me there would be an archbishop to greet me."

He inquired how things where in our lovely little town that he will always call home. We went inside,

"Would you like something to drink?"

"Yes, a beer."

"Father Joseph told me that you might say a beer he also filled me in why he sent you to see me. So, if you're ready to start, fire away, like Father Joseph told you do not be shy or ashamed to talk to me. I hope I can take away the confusion on certain topics. I am listening."

"Well, where do I start when you discussed with Father Joseph the reason for my being here today. Did he mention my encounter with the black mass with the red eyes and everything that has been happening since that Monday night?"

"Yes he did, you invited the black mass into your world."

"With all due respect, I did not invite anybody."

"Yes, you did by being so cocky challenging them to come and see that you were not afraid and would be able to put them in their place, strong words my friend. An entity will always respond to a challenge."

"I still do not know why everyone keeps on reminding me that I was cocky? I disagree with that notion, I was being honest about not believing in the paranormal that's why I was always telling people that I was not afraid and would be able to handle myself against an entity."

"Okay, okay, slow down please."

"Sorry, but I truly believed that it was all make believe and the chance that something would happen was like a snowball's chance in hell."

"Alright, no need to get so uptight. That's the impression that you were giving with your trash talk. Anyway moving forward, did your mom talk to you about being native… you know, first nation."

"Yes."

"You must know by now that native people are very spiritual and strongly believe in reincarnation, talking to the dead, asking the elders for guidance and protection."

"Yes I know all about that."

"Father Joseph told me that you have questions about you being an Indigo child."

"Yes, why me? Why choose me?"

"Did Father Joseph talk to you about your sixth sense?"

"If he did, I do not remember. I was extremely nervous while talking to him. It's possible that I may have missed some information."

"Did Father Joseph mentioned anything regarding your near death accident?"

"Yes he did, I do not like it. I still think there must have been a better way to let me know instead of that morbid situation. A letter or a phone call would have been sufficient."

"Good, your still cracking jokes. That Monday night was only the beginning, do you still see the black entity or feel his presence?"

"Yes, I cannot shake it off."

"Of course,he is also here for a purpose. Growing up, do you remember noticing a lot of feathers of different colors on the ground, pointing in different directions?"

"Yes."

"The feathers where sent to you by your elders for you to understand the dangers, consequences about the way you where dismissing, laughing and the most dangerous daring the spirits, entities to come and see you. That's the worst thing that you could have done."

"Yes, I know I have been told more than once, that my attitude towards the spirits was not a good one."

"You were lucky not to get hurt. I know about a case similar to yours that the individual was actually attacked by the entities. The victim suffered numerous injuries and also affected the victim's mental health."

"I am not worried."

"You should be worried and be careful on what you say or do. I could tell you a lot more of what I have seen over the years, but you are not here to talk about someone else's misfortunes."

"That's right. "

"Alright before we continue, do you need a break?"

"No, thank you. I am okay for now."

"Okay, then let's continue. You probably have seen strange things, hearing voices in the past few months?"

"Yes I have, it's driving me crazy."

"The reasons for my questions is because your near death opened a door that you kept shut without knowing anything about the door."

"I know Father Joseph told me the same thing that you are telling me."

"All the things that are now happening is because of who you are."

"You say because of who I am, but why then when growing up, why did my spirit did not let me know? And why was I given a personality that did not believe in any of that stuff?"

"At birth you are given a soul, the rest is up to you. They cannot control the brain or the heart of a person. You have to follow the road in front of you and make sure that you make the right decisions along the way."

"I don't quite understand what you're trying to tell me."

"Let me tell you something before we continue, it might help you to better understand what I am trying to tell you. Did you know some souls get trapped between this world and the spiritual world? They can get confused and very angry. They can cause havoc trying to understand why they are stuck in the middle of nowhere."

"That's why there are so many spirits in limbo."

"I am going to tell you a story about a family that did not listen to other people's warnings not to go and visit a cemetery that is known for its restless and lost souls."

"Is it a true story?"

"Yes, a true story. They paid the price, some souls followed them home. A family of four, one girl, one boy, mom and dad. The young girl did not want to go so she stayed behind, but that did not matter to the souls if she stayed home."

"Spirits were looking to retaliate because the family invaded their space."

"That's right... so that night at home, the young girl was going upstairs to her room, she was pushed down the stairs by an entity and broke her back."

"Wow, the spirits were that physical."

"Yes they were. Fortunately for her she was able to make a full recovery. The young man was possessed by a spirit. The boy needed help from a priest to perform an exorcism for the spirit to release his hold on the young boy."

"Really an exorcism wow that's serious shit man."

"The boy has not been the same since the possession of the spirit. He is struggling with depression, the mother who was taking the pictures that night, her case was the worst."

"How can it be worst than being possessed?"

"She is now in a mental institution, the dad cannot hold a steady job. He is living with a dark rage inside of him that he cannot escape from."

"The whole family is now damaged goods."

"That's right, the kids live in a foster home. You see like you said they invaded their territory, so the souls invaded the family's territory they made sure the family paid the price for disturbing them."

"Wow, quite the story."

"Yes, it is quite the story. Unfortunately, a story based on true events. That's when you come in. An indigo child sees the world in a different way that we do. Let me explain what I mean by telling you that you see the world in a different way."

"Yes, please."

"You are able to communicate with the spirit world, through several channels, spirits will come to see you for guidance. What I mean by that you will guide the spirit to heaven."

"How am I supposed to do that?"

"No need to worry. When the time comes, you will know what to do. Indigo children are born with the knowledge and methods to tackle situations that will come their way. When the spirits are ready to leave our world, they go join their loved ones in heaven."

"Excuse me but your phone is ringing."

"I will be right back."

"Take your time, I am not going anywhere."

While the archbishop was on the phone, it gave me a little bit of time to try to absorb all the information that was given by the archbishop.

After a few minutes the archbishop made his way back to me.

"Okay were was I?"

"You were standing right in front of me."

"Thank you for reminding me you little smartass."

"You're welcome."

"Okay let's continue. You will see a white light shaped about the size of a ping pong ball coming towards you. You will go into a trance and accompany the soul to the gates of heaven and then be yourself again."

"Really, that's what I will need to do on a daily basis. What if I do not want like you said do the work, can I block the whole thing and go on with my life. Why was I given this so-called gift without asking me if I would accept this?"

"No, you were not given the chance to refuse. Going forward this is what you will have to do almost daily."

"I do not call that a gift, it's going to cause me some agony, stress and I will not be able to live a normal life. Everybody should be able to fend for themselves."

"And no you cannot close the doors… why ask, you already know the answer?"

"What will happen if I mess up the first couple of times that I am needed to perform my duty. Are they going to revoke… you know, my gift and give it to someone else? I might be selfish but I want to live a regular life like everybody else."

"Boy, I did not expect this kind of reaction."

"I am sorry but it's my life that we are talking about. If I do what I have to do is it going to give me a free ride to heaven?"

"It should give you a free ride to heaven."

"What do you mean it should, you're not certain?"

"Okay, I have enough of this nonsense now listen to me we could talk until we are both blue in the face it's not going to change anything. It's a gift that was given to you by God and it was given to you for a reason. It's a gift that you do not unwrap on Christmas eve.

"I do know that it's not a gift that I can unwrap Christmas eve."

"If you do not change your attitude this conversation is over. I am not here to argue with you, I am here to help you and if I cannot do that, you are wasting my time. Talk about an irrational behavior."

"I am sorry, I apologize, it was not my intention to cause you any grief when you mentioned a gift from God. It made me realise that God put his faith in me and that I can be trusted."

"That's right and no need to apologize."

"Wow that's a special privilege that not too many people have. I will roll up my sleeves and do my best to accomplish what needs to be done."

"I understand that it's a big responsibility that was given to you and do not worry about making mistakes, we all make mistakes."

"I do not want to let anybody down, I will do my best. I hope that the situations won't be too stressfull. I have a question, someone told me if you have a near-death experience your soul leaves your body, another soul takes its place. Someone told me that I do not have the same soul that I was born with?"

"The Catholic church does not believe in that fact. Your soul does not leave your body because you are not dead, like the words say near death."

"What about the ones that die and after a few minutes they come back, do they still have the same soul?"

"Yes, because they are going towards heaven and they decided to come back."

"I have a few more questions if you do not mind?"

"Of course not."

"Will I have to deal with the souls of individuals who died and after a few minutes they come back to life?"

"No the spirit will go back to the body."

"Thank you. I now have a pretty good idea what to expect. One last question about reincarnation, how do the souls know when babies are born which soul for which baby? Nobody can answer my question."

"Some souls will remain in heaven for a long period of time, some stay in heaven indefinitely, some reincarnate in a short period of time. When a future mom is pregnant a soul will attach itself to the fetus of the unborn baby that the spirit has chosen."

"How does the process work regarding the birth of so many babies?"

"That I do not know they have some kind of system. Do you know, we do not die we transform it's not a body with a spirit, it's a spirit with a body, for the spirit we are like a suitcase."

"Do you know why some spirits haunt instead of making their way to heaven?"

"Sometimes when a person dies for example in a car accident they do not realize they are dead, they can also be victims of violence that cost them their lives."

"So in an unexpected situation they are confused."

"Not all of them and as I was saying, they want their story heard and justice done, some are so attached to their house, belongings, they simply do not want to leave. If you have a chance look inside an empty church, it's full of spirits that are lost or looking for redemption."

"Like you previously said they are trapped between two worlds, something like your cemetery story."

"Yes, I guess in a way you can say that, but not all the cases are the same. One question, is this your final year of high school?"

"Yes, why?"

"Just curious if you have made a decision which career path you are going to take."

"I have, I want to be a firefighter."

"Good choice, anything else I can help you with today?"

"No, you have been a great help. I now understand what to expect. Thank you."

"I hope I was able to remove roadblocks on your highway of life. If you have a chance, take a close look at the tree of life; you might be surprised what you will see. The leaves never fall from the tree, the branches never move even in a wind storm."

"Where can I see the tree of life? "

"You cannot physically see the tree. For different cultures, the tree of life is a different shape and size but the meaning of the tree remains the same.

"Where can I get information on the tree?"

"The best place to look for information about the tree is on the internet (Wikipedia- the free encyclopedia) and religious books. Good luck! Remember if you need help, the church will always be there to help you."

(The tree of life is a fundamental archetype in many of the worlds-- mythologies, religious and philosophical traditions. It is closely related to the concept of the sacred tree. The tree of knowledge, connecting to heaven and the underworld and the tree of life, connecting all forms of creation, are both forms of the world tree or cosmic tree and are portrayed in various religions and philosophies as the same tree.)

I went home with a lot more confidence, understanding of what to expect and what I will need to do. I never though in a million years that it would be so demanding and affect my everyday life.

I better prepare myself because this is only the beginning. When I arrived home, my mom was waiting for me with a list of questions. To her surprise, I was able to answer every questions.

"I am proud of you. I know that everyday, you will do whatever it takes to get things done."

After graduating from high school, I went to college. After two years of hard work, another graduation, I am now a firefighter; some days were more challenging than others, studying for exams and dealing with situations at the same time.

A note about situations, I cannot write about them all, way too many I would still be writing. The cases and events in this book are the ones that really stood out for me.

To have the ability to travel from one dimension to another dimension… to be able to see the spirit world is truly amazing.

I was very fortunate to be able to join my hometown fire department. Like it's often the case for new graduates, they have to take a job until they can get their foot in the door of a fire station.

Some go on a waiting list or take a position with a fire department away from home. I guess for me it was meant to be.

My mom was always worried, afraid that one day there will be a situation that I would not be able to handle. She knew that I would take risks, take a big bite that was too big to chew. She would always say.

"Be careful to try and do something which is way over your head. I am afraid that you might get hurt with severe injuries or even worst and also have an impact on your mental state of mind."

"I know Mom."

"It's great that you are able to help a lot of people but I wish god would have chosen someone else. I might be selfish by saying that, you're my son. I have a hard time to accept that maybe one day I will get a phone call."

"I can understand mom why you worry so much, but I am here for a reason. I will be around for a very long time."

"You're a firefighter-- one of the most dangerous jobs in the world."

"I know Mom but trust me I am not going anywhere anytime soon. I am too much of a pain in the ass to make a quick exit from this life."

"A pain in the ass is putting it lightly. I do trust you but as a mother I cannot help it to worry."

The people that came to me for answers about their loved ones that passed away did everything go as planned when he/she entered heaven.

I always advise the person that I am providing details on how it went and to keep the information for themselves because I want to keep it quiet, low key as possible.

Some do keep it to themselves, but for some it's impossible not to talk about what I did or said. They cannot wait to tell family, friends. We humans, we are born to gossip we feed on it, it's in our blood.

One subject of discussion is my voice. They say that I have a very calming voice and they feel comfortable with me and able to talk without prejudice. They know that I am trustworthy. They know everything they tell me will stay with me because it's nobody else's business. The fact they trust me is great. My lips are sealed.

Since my near death episode people are still inquiring if I saw a light or something like the golden doors, dead relatives, family members.

One of my friends wanted to know why I do it for free.

"Why do you not charge a fee to the ones you help? You could make some easy money."

"I deal more with souls than the living. I will certainly not charge a fee for answering a few questions in their time of need, most of the time they ask me questions that I cannot answer. For some people like you it's always about the money, pockets full of money and cold empty hearts."

"As a friend it is not a very nice thing to say to me."

"Well, as a friend you should know not to ask me that type of question. You know I thought you knew me better than that, and not ask me such a question"

"You are right, I am sorry to ask you such a dumb question. I was only looking after your best interest."

"I am sorry for being rude and thank you for looking after my best interest if I ever need help, I will let you know."

"That's okay, I deserved it. You are right, I should have known better to ask you such a question."

We shook hands. Everyday, the questions keep on coming.

One night, I woke up floating above my bed a few inches from the ceiling. I could hear music and monks humming as if they were in a church praying. I slowly descended back on my bed.

I squeezed my nose, my cheek to make sure I was not sleeping. I sat on the side of the bed for a few minutes, I made my way to the kitchen to get a glass of water, went back to bed. Everything was quiet, my wife was still asleep.

I was not able to go back to sleep. I was trying to understand why or for what reason I was floating, to me it did not make any sense and also the music and the humming.

I was awake for a few hours, everything remained silent and I finally fell asleep. In the morning, I asked my wife if she heard music and humming in the middle of the night.

"No. Why are you asking me such a question?"

"I woke up floating over my bed and monks humming and I could hear music."

"Are you sure? It could have been a dream."

"I know that it was not a dream. I will go see Father Joseph."

"Are you leaving now?"

"In a few minutes, I am anxious to hear what he has to say."

So I made my way to Father Joseph residence and knocked on the door. When he answered the door, he was not surprised it was me.

"Come in, I was wondering when I would see you again. What can I help you with today?"

After filling him in for the reason for my visit and if he had any idea or explanation for what I just told him. He looked baffled.

"Good question."

"Yes indeed. I am baffled, I cannot think of anything unless they were trying to send you a message for a reason I do not know."

"They could use e-mail to send me messages, but seriously maybe they were trying to tell me that I am not alone to do battles with black entities."

"Could be, I do not know but one thing that I do know is that you interfere with their work. The entities are here for only one reason, they want to lure every soul to hell."

"I put up a wall between the souls and the entities."

"That's right, you are preventing them to lure the souls towards them. You are in their way and they do not like it. You know everywhere you go, you will be on a battlefield."

"I know. But I hope that I can once in a while leave the battlefield. Thank you again for your help. I am sure we will talk again."

"I am sure we will and sorry for the lack of information. If I find an answer to your question, I will let you know."

The spirits/souls come to me for guidance. I tell my wife that unfortunately someone will pass away within a few days. When the time comes, the soul will come to see me so that I can guide him to heaven.

"I know it's hard for you to understand but it's a feeling that I get."

One thing that really gets to me is when people want straight answers which I always provide. If they do not like my answers and don't tell them what they want to hear, they become nasty, or rude.

Some say I do not know what I am talking about. I always reply if you did not want to hear the truth why bother to ask and waste my time, but the majority do accept their fate or the fate of their loved ones.

I know critics will say they can debunk all the facts. Well good luck boys. You cannot debunk all events in the world. They need to learn that we are surrounded by angels and demons.

Evil entities are fallen angels who had a fallout with God. Remember, ghosts were once people like me and you.

The black entity that was in my room that fateful night has been following me for years. Sometimes he brings a friend along with him. I guess to try to prove a point, I do not know for me it does not change anything.

I keep on doing what needs to be done. Maybe he wants to learn by watching me . Maybe he wants to become an indigo demon. Who knows? Sometimes I come face to face with my faithful followers. I look in their red eyes, lower my head and keep going.

My so called side job brings a burden to my family. I feel guilty for what they have to go through because of me. People keep bothering them with questions. People will point their finger and say he is one of his siblings, go ask him or her a question about their brother. They get a lot of prank calls but not as much as I do.

I always hang up, I have no time to waste on ridiculous comments from stupid people. I do not get lured in and play their game.

I wear a chain around my neck with a cross as a pendant that was given to me by my daughter. The cross was dipped in holy water and blessed by a priest.

I have been told by many know it all who think they have an answer for everything, I call them bunkhouse lawyers that I do not need the cross because I am fake, I am the type of person that is always looking for attention.

One time I put one of the bunkhouse lawyers to the test. I let him waste his saliva. He was trying to impress a small group of people with his comments.

"You done? Now it`s my turn to talk. What makes you an expert? I sure would like to see your diploma and what facts do you have to back your comments? Do you have any literature that we could read and educate ourselves?"

"Okay, okay I get the message."

"Do you know what I call guys like you that try to impress people with their dumb comments, or attitude? I call them bunkhouse lawyers, now put that in your pipe and smoke it. I wonder which one of us that our small audience think who is the idiot?"

He looked at me with a surprised angry look. I could hear individuals laugh, telling jokes aimed at him. He did not say another word, he made his way to his car with his head between his legs.

The small group dispersed, some congratulated me, some said *well done he deserved it.* I hope he learned a lesson to make him think twice before trying to make fun of someone . I said thank you and I drove home.

My daughter noticed black shadows in her room that kept bothering her. I yelled.

"Leave her alone! Your fight is not with her, it`s with me. Cowards going after my daughter instead of me. I know why you idiots are afraid to face me because I can defend myself. I would be ashamed, in real life all of you must have been mama`s boy."

I was pushed hard enough for me to fall backwards. Thank god they decided to leave her alone and concentrate more on me. I did not know at the time that I was in for a heck of a ride.

One thing that I need to mention is that when I lend a hand to my friends, neighbors and strangers, helping my fellow man always makes me feel good; but the feeling is always short lived because of all the bad luck that comes my way.

I feel as if I am punished for doing good deeds, so I went to see my fountain of information Father Joseph if he could shed some light on why all the bad luck that comes my way.

He was waiting for me at the door, it was nighttime. When he opened the door to let me in, it was dark he could clearly see a white light, an aura around me.

"Come in, the last time you were here, did I mention there`s a white light around you?

"No, you did not."

"Because it`s dark outside I was able to get a better look."

"If that's the case, why would the archbishop not tell me?"

"Was it daytime when you went to see him?"He probably did not see the light because it was daytime, take me for example it's the first time that I can see the light because like I said it's dark outside."

"So father you're telling me that a light is always shining around me.

"That's right."

"What is the meaning of that light, how come myself and other people cannot see it?"

"The reason for the light is to guide the spirits towards you. It is a light that can only be seen by a selected few individuals."

"Wow, does that mean that I am a saint?"

"Oh god, no you a saint I will not call you a saint.. I will not go that far not just yet."

"A light around me I wish that the light would be powerful enough for me to use at night. I could use it in the house and save on my hydro consumption and save money. My wife keeps telling me that I have hair on my back shaped like wings."

"Really let me see. I will be darned she is right."

"No kidding. My wife was not joking when she told me about my wings. How bizarre it's probably a coincidence."

"Not really, it's who you are."

"I don't quite understand when people say it's who you are. I am an ordinary guy like everybody else but with a few perks. I do not like it when people say it's because of who you are. There are a lot more powerful human beings on this earth compared to me."

"We are not talking about everybody else, we are talking about you."

"Sorry for my babbling. If I put my wings to good use I could become a flying porch light maybe that's why in some of my dreams, I can fly a short distance at a very low level… like they say in the military 'fly under the radar'."

"I am sure that you did not come here to talk about the hair on your back . What's up?"

"I am here today because I cannot understand all the bad luck I am having. It's ridiculous, very annoying."

"Bad luck."

"Yes, bad luck. There is always something to ruin my day or weekend. If I was to tell my friends about all the bad luck they probably will not believe me. It's crazy, it's driving me bananas."

"What is your date of birth?"

I told him my age. He retrieved a book from one of the shelves, shuffled a few pages."

"Sit down, this might take a while."

With the information in the book, Father Joseph did a karmic auscultation.

"You are not responsible for what is happening to you. You simply carry what is called karmic debt that you inherited from birth, this produces some sort of occult; adversity that cause a threat or failure and bad luck to hover you permanently it is as if you have to pay a high price for an error that you did not commit."

"can I see the book please."

"You need to understand karmic debt. The physics of karma, action-reaction, energy and karmic debt… here, read what is written in the book."

He gave me the book and in the content of the book,

(It is said that all the action-reaction-responses that we experience in life are from the force of karmic debt accumulations (karma quotient) these are said to include the results of all activities that one does in any state, whether in knowledge, ignorance or by chance, accident or otherwise in other words all work, activity or energy debts are karmic (action) debts.)

This necessarily mean out of accumulations of action-reaction, the individual consciousness needs to"reincarnate" since the results of the debts cannot balance out in a lifetime scientific proof of reincarnation as been proven. So, there you go… very well explained.

"Thank you for letting me read some of the book's content. I noticed there is no title on the cover of the book, how come?"

"For some reason, the author did not want for the book to have a title. Have you also noticed no mention as to who wrote the book?"

"Strange. Anyway, I will do more research on the subject. Thank you Father. Talk to you soon."

"You're welcome. Do me a favor please on way out can you lock the door for me. Turn the little gadget to the right and when you close the door it will automatically lock the door. Thank you."

"One more question before I leave, it's not easy that I can predict something is going to happen. Unfortunately, I cannot see when or where it will take place. I am close to ninety nine percent when it comes to my predictions."

"That's a good average."

"Yes, too good of an average for my liking. For example, in the news there was an industrial accident; ten employees dead, shootings in the work place, concerts, these are only a few of many predictions. Is there a way that I can block the predictions for these events?"

"You can try but I am afraid you will not be able to do so, unless you try to block everything else that is happening."

"No, I do not want to do that. One more thing that I need to mention, I am not the only one at home that can hear voices, able to see spirits, entities, my wife is what you call a sensitive. Imagine our topics of discussions."

"I can well imagine."

"Thanks again Father for your time and putting up with me."

"You are very welcome. See you later."

One question that comes up the most is it true when you commit suicide you do not go to heaven?"

"Go talk to a priest he might have an answer because I am not sure myself."

I never see spirits from people who commit suicide. I did my own research on the subject and the answer is, no they do not go to heaven. They go to another dimension because you should not take a life even if it's your own. That's the biggest sin that a human being can do take a life.

I went back the following day to again to talk to Father Joseph. When he answered the door, his first words were…

"Well, well who we have here. I think that I recognize you from yesterday am, am I right?"

"Haha very funny, you're the one that told me the door will always be open if I need a help or information."

"I know, I am only pulling your leg come in. What's up?"

"One thing that I wanted to talk to you yesterday and it slipped my mind is the fact that I have been invited several times to participate in a seance. I always decline their invitation, I feel they do more harm than good."

"Yes, stay away from seances, they are dangerous. I have seen what a seance can do, it's not pretty. I get a lot of individuals who participated and they all need help for one reason or another, so stay away."

"Will do, thanks. That's all for today again thank you for your time Father. Like they say in french *a la prochaine mon ami* ."

"Yes until next time take care, be careful."

Chapter 5

I have learned to be patient, because patience was not one of my strong points. When I would ask god a question, I wanted an answer, asap. Father Joseph educated me to be patient. When the time comes, I will get my answer.

On occasions, I go to a silent place where I can be by myself, ask god a question regarding circumstances that I do not understand.

Archangel Michael provides me the answers to my questions. If your question remains unanswered, watch for events, situations that will answer your question. Patience is a virtue.

The reason Father Joseph wants to stay in touch is he wants updates on how my patience is progressing. He once told me that the public trust me, I should do more volunteer work. It will keep my mind occupied and be more patient with the public.

I now understand it all makes sense. He does not want me to have a temper tantrum when things go wrong, make a fool of myself and lose the public's trust.

Like I mentioned earlier in the book, I can sense, predict certain circumstances that will cause grief for the person/persons involved, also the outcome for someone battling a disease or complicated surgeries.

One of my friends took a vacation in a third world country. While on vacation, he caught a virus and became gravely ill. He spent over a month in a hospital until he was well enough to fly home. His doctor diagnosed his disease and informed my friend that he needed a long, risky surgery because the virus spread to his internal organs.

My friend was extremely nervous which is natural for that type of situation. He came over to my house and wanted some insight regarding his surgery. I put my hand on his shoulder.

"Look into my eyes and listen to what I have to say. We've been friends for a very long time and you trust me right?"

"Yes, you know I trust you."

"No need to worry, the surgery will be a success. You will be fine and back home in no time."

The surgery was a success, he returned to work sooner than expected. He said that he kept repeating what I said, that he felt safe and confident on his way to surgery. His wife told me that she was pessimistic about what I said to her husband.

"What you told him gave him a world of confidence. On his way to surgery he kept repeating what you said. What you said really helped to boost his confidence. I am grateful, thank you, when it comes to your prediction. I am still a bit skeptical, the jury is still out on that one."

"You know in your heart, we have been friends for so many years since high school. I would not say that everything will be fine if I was not sure, put our friendship in jeopardy giving him false hope."

"I guess your right, I should know by now not to doubt you, and again thank you very much."

"You're welcome but the ones you should be thanking are the doctors and nurses. They did all the leg work. I only told him what I saw, the rest was in god's hand."

My former boss was fighting a losing battle with cancer. The doctor told him there was nothing they could do for him. He called and invited me for a cup of coffee. He told me what the doctor said that nothing else could be done for him.

He wanted an idea of how much time he had left. The doctor told him about ten months. He greeted me with a smile. We sat down at the kitchen table, his wife was a mess; she could not accept the fact that he will be gone in a matter of months.

"The doctor told me about ten months but I also want your input. My wife wants to know if there is a chance they will be able to celebrate one more family Christmas with me."

I put my hand on his shoulder and closed my eyes.

"I see snow because it's winter time then grass and again snow. The last thing that I can see is snow and mud which means spring time."

He celebrated his last christmas with the whole family including brothers, sisters, grandkids, nephews,nieces ect. He wanted his last Christmas to be remembered by everyone. He died early April.

A small group of the town's population think that I can perform miracles. They want me to prevent them from dying. I keep repeating over and over that I am unable to perform miracles, they should be talking to god not me.

Some get upset with me, thinking I did not want to take the time and effort to help them. A mother begged me to do or say something to prevent her daughter from dying. Her daughter was diagnosed with level four stomach cancer. Her daughter only had a short time to live. She offered me a ton of money. Again, I had to tell a mother that I could not help her. She looked at me.

"I am so sorry but there is nothing I can do, but pray and ask god for more time."

I could hear her sobbing until she drove away. One day, a young man approached me and punched me in the face because I did not give him proper information for his mom.

"Remember me, your good at lying to people."

"Listen and listen carefully to what I am going to tell you. Your lucky that I did not defend myself or press charges against you for assault. I know that you are upset, sometimes things can change, I have no control over that."

"Why things change?"

"It`s god`s decision not mine. Maybe your mom talked to god, asked him to come and get her, she could not take the pain and suffering anymore."

"I doubt that."

"Besides, I never told your mom that I was one hundred percent accurate, otherwise it would mean that I would have a hundred percent batting average which would be a perfect batting average. That`s impossible because perfection does not exist."

He looked at me, shrugged his shoulders, gave me the finger before getting in his car. Events like this one, and confrontations really elevated my stress level. My friend suggested that I go see a therapist. I took his advice. My first session was very mellow. I was shy because the therapist was a woman. I did not have any choice, she was the only one accepting new patients.

I did not know how to approach her for certain things that I wanted to talk about. My second visit, she made me feel more at home, I was a lot more comfortable which made it easier to discuss certain subjects that I was reluctant to talk about in my first session.

"Are you aware that I am an indigo child?"

"No, you did not mention it in our first session that you were an indigo child. With this new information for me, we will have to take a different approach in order for me to be able to help you."

I was able to take a load off my shoulders by talking nonstop for almost an hour. She took notes as I went along. I also mentioned the fact that I am native and I communicate with my elders using feathers, about our medicine wheel which she found very fascinating.

I also mentioned the high level of stress that I was feeling, having to deal with people, spirits and harmful entities. My third visit, my therapist said since talking to me about feathers, she now sees a a lot of them with different colors, pointing in different directions before talking to me she never noticed, paid any attention to feathers that was on the ground.

"I was feeling blue, I went for a walk. I noticed a feather descending in front of me. Do you know what that means?"

"Are you aware if you have native blood flowing in your veins?"

"No, I do not have any native blood flowing in my veins."

"Okay, well the feather was probably for someone else."

"Are you sure? Because as far as I could see, there was no one else on the sidewalk."

"Was it breezy that day?"

"Yes, it was."

"The feather was floating in the wind and did not land where it was supposed to land."

My sessions were starting to pay off. Everything was starting to fall into place and making sense. My following visit, I described her house. She was amazed how accurate I was with the details. The reason that I was able to describe her home was because when she walked into her office, I had a vision of cardboard boxes.

"My son is moving to be closer to a hospital. He was diagnosed with blood deficiency problems. He cannot be more than thirty minutes from the hospital.

She asked me the dreaded question.

"Is he going to be okay?"

"I put my hand on her shoulder, now think only about your son."

She closed her eyes and concentrated real hard only of her son. I was able to see the outcome of her son. I removed my hand from her shoulder.

"I cannot tell you if he will ever be okay, but what I can tell you is this. He will be among the living for quite some time to come. But one thing that, I want you to understand what I see, things may change. I have no control over the situation, I am not always hundred percent about my visions but close."

"I understand, thank you. Now let`s talk about you and see if we can make any progress today."

The following session, the therapist was running late. When she arrived, I told her the reason why she was late.

"A relative passed away, the funeral was this morning."

"Goodness you never miss a beat."

"I wish I could skip a beat. Believe me, I have tried many times with no success."

That was my final weekly session, now I go see my therapist once a month. She provided me with the necessary tools, methods to help me cope. I am happy that my therapist believes in the paranormal, because today I might be in the loony bin.

Not only do I have to deal with events almost everyday. Remember, earlier in the book, I wrote that I wanted a minimum of people to know what I am able to do. As the years go by, my secret is shrinking on a daily basis.

I am not a fool. I knew my privacy would diminish with every situation. Well one of my friends contacted a television station to set up an interview with me to talk about my sixth sense.

What a surprise when a representative from the television station called to schedule a interview with me. I declined the interview, I advised the person I was talking with, not to say a word and not mention my name. He responded.

"Freedom of the press."

I requested to talk to the station manager. I made him understand that I was going to deny everything and whatever the question I would reply *no* and that my friends pulled a prank on the television station and how silly the station would look.

He told me not to worry he did not want to spend time and money on a dead horse. I thanked him and hung up the phone. Boy what a relief, that was a close call, I can just imagine the interview being blown out of proportion in the newpaper, on social media. The pesky reporters wanting a story.

As for my friend, I have not spoken a word to him since the television station called to set up that famous interview.

I later found out that television stations pay the indidvidual who brings a story or news to be aired on television. My friend called several times to talk and also apologize. I told him that he was not trustworthy to be my friend. I would not be able to trust him anymore.

"You went behind my back and tried to make money at my expense, do you know the publicity that would have been generated? I would have been skinned alive. The level of stress a lot of grief and most of all unwanted attention."

"I told you several times that I am sorry."

"You need to learn to keep your mouth shut or else I will install a zipper over your mouth, put a lock on it, that way you will not be able to open your loud mouth. When meal time comes, a straw will be a utensil."

Black entities were invading my house. Father Joseph came over to bless the house. While he was going from room to room with his crucifix and holy water. I was following him with burning sage and a feather to spread the smoke of the burning sage in every room.

Father Joseph also put some salt on every window sills and door frames. The house was quiet for a short period of time before the entities came back. They are like an army unit; they retreat, regroup and again go on the offensive, sometimes I do not see it coming. They use the element of surprise.

Although I should be, I am never prepared to tackle surprises. I have to reach down in my bag of ideas to improvise in resolving the issues. I have to admit some cases take an emotional toll on me.

The candle factory must love me, to relax after a long difficult day. I relax by sitting in the dark, light white candles and I look at the reflection of the burning candles on the wall which helps me to relax, the burning candles are also removing bad vibes in the house .

Chapter 6

Almost every day, I deal with the paranormal at home. One afternoon, a young girl, I would say between eight or ten years old, was standing in front of the kitchen window looking outside. She turned her head, looked at me and disappeared.

One night, I avoided an attack from behind, from an entity by turning my head in his direction. He vanished. I am sure he wanted to push me down the basement stairs as I was going down the stairs with a box in my hands. One night, I was tossing and turning in bed. I could not sleep.

I could feel a presence in the room, I was right. I was punched real hard on the shoulder by an invisible entity. The next morning, I could see a bruise on my shoulder. My shoulder hurt for several days. One morning, I woke up with the sensation of bugs crawling all over my body. Thank god, the bugs were not for real.

One night when we went to bed, there was a strong smell of urine coming from the bed even after changing the sheets we could still smell urine coming from the bed. We closed our bedroom door behind us and went to sleep in the guess room. The following morning, I opened our bedroom door, the smell was gone.

I looked at my wife.

"Maybe last night, there were two entities lying on our bed and they were too shy to use the bathroom."

"Very funny. "

One evening when we came home after a day of shopping, two entities were sitting on the couch, a young man and a young woman holding hands, they smiled and vanished. That same evening, we could see two entities walking in the hallway and disappear.

I popped the question to Father Joseph if he knew the reason why there were so many ghosts walking in the house and then disappear.

"They are probably using the same portal, the black entities use to go back and forth. They are just passing through. They mean no harm."

"I cannot understand why there would be a portal in my house. I built my house myself and with help from a few friends. There was no sign of any portal."

"The portal was opened that Monday night."

"But it`s not in the same house. "

"It does not matter, the portal will follow you no matter where you go. "

"Really? Oh boy, is there a way to close the portal?"

"If you close that one, they will open another one. As long as you keep guiding souls to heaven, they will always bring the fight to you."

"Does that mean the boogeyman with the red eyes will pay me another visit in the middle of the night?"

"It's a possibility."

"I am not happy to hear that but okay I guess I will have to live with it. Thanks again, Father."

Earlier in the book, I mentioned that I am a recipient of bad luck. I am the king of mishaps. Since me and my better half met, she is also plagued with bad luck. Before we met, she was never involved in a car accident.

Since we tied the knot, she has been involved in four car accidents. Thank god, only minor injuries. She suffered major injuries when she fell off her horse . She spent five days in an intensive care unit with a total of eighteen days in the hospital. She has been in and out of the hospital several times for different medical issues.

My niece is a clairvoyant, she predicted that I would injure my back while fighting a house fire. She was right. People kept pestering her with a thousand and one questions, if they purchase a lottery ticket will they win? Will they win the big prize playing bingo?

Some individuals kept nagging her about their future. Too many people asking too many questions so she shut it down. She was able to block the visions and so forth. One night, she came over for a visit and saw numerous shadow spirits. The only visions she could not block are visions of shadows and spirits. She was frightened when she spotted a demon entity lurking in the basement.

"Well uncle, it's time for me to go home."

"You saw something that scared you."

"Yes, a demon entity in the basement."

My wife was puzzled because she was not able to see any spirits and the demonic entity.

"I am supposed to be a sensitive and tonight I was not able to see nothing out of the ordinary. I don't understand."

"You can only see the ones that want to be seen. Well, goodnight and thank you for the lovely evening. Love you both."

One of my friends, I have way too many friends, so anyway, his wife was going through a very difficult pregnancy. He was worried for both his wife and the baby. By chance, we ran into each other at the grocery store. I could see that worried look on his face. He was happy to see me. He said that he was stressed out and worried.

"Her due date is in a couple of weeks. The doctors mentioned that it will be a very difficult birth. They may have to do a c-section."

I did my usual ritual by putting my hand on his shoulder. He was relieved when I told him everything will be fine.

"To be honest, yes it's going to be a complicated delivery; but everything will turn out okay for both the mom and the baby."

"Running into each other today is no coincidence."

"What do you mean?"

"It was meant for us to meet to talk about the birth of our baby."

"What makes you say that?"

"It's because of who you are."

"I am starting to despise those word."

"Really? Okay, well, you are at the store to buy groceries not to meet up with me. What are the odds that we would bump into each other? It was planned by the powers above. They wanted you to reassure me to take a load of worry off my back."

"I do not see it that way. For me it's a coincidence."

"It's not a coincidence. Stop being so modest and accept who you are, anyway, I need to go. I will let you know when the baby is born and how it went. Thanks, man. Talk to you soon."

A few weeks later he came over to the house with a beaming smile and a grin from ear to ear.

"When my wife was in labor, I was nervous as hell, worried and you popped into my head until my son was born. She gave birth with no major issues. They are both doing great. Thank you, thank you, thank you, my friend I will always be grateful."

"I only reassured you that everything would be fine. Your wife deserves all the credit."

"I know but still you gave us a lot of confidence. I think you know more than you let on."

"I do not have anything to do with the outcome. I only tell people what I feel or see; that's all, nothing else. I do not have any magical or special powers."

"I am not so sure about that."

He gave me a hug and a cigar. He looked at his watch.

"I better get going. I have a full box of cigars that needs to be emptied."

And he was on his way.

My dad's best friend died at the tender age of thirty-nine due to massive heart attack. They worked together, hunted and fished together. They were best buddies, inseparable, they were like brothers. They would hang out in my dad's backyard garage. They would work on small projects and shared the cost of the tools.

When his friend died, my dad was not able to go in the garage until all of his best friend's stuff was taken away. One night, my dad and my uncle were in the garage having a conversation. All of a sudden, tools started flying in the air. Pictures on the walls started to shake, my uncle looked at my dad with a puzzled look on his face.

"No need to worry. It's my best friend who passed away manifesting his presence."

The event really shook my uncle. Even today, he still talks about that evening in the garage. Paranormal activity can happen to every one of us. All over the world, there are thousands of witnesses of the paranormal that do not come forward to talk about their encounter.

They are afraid to be ridiculed by the public. Some witnesses do not see any reasons to report the events. The non -believers, well that`s another story altogether.

One of my friend`s brother-in-law passed away, also from a massive heart attack. My friend was at work and a sensation came over him to look up at the sky and he started to pray. He recited prayers until the sensation was gone. He talked to Father Joseph about that day. Father Joseph told him his brother-in-law reached out to him. He needed prayers to be able to enter in heaven.

My dad`s mom, my grandmother was capable to stop someone from bleeding. One day, my grandfather had a heavy nosebleed. The blood was coming out of both nostrils as if someone opened the kitchen faucets. My grandfather had high blood pressure; veins ruptured in both nostrils.

My grandmother was able to slow down the bleeding but unsuccessful to completely stop the bleeding altogether. The effort to stop the bleeding was starting to take its toll on my grandmother. She was getting weak.

The doctor's office was forty miles away. A few minutes before reaching the doctor's office, my grandmother passed out. My uncle rushed my grandfather into the doctor's office; he ran back to the car to attend to my grandmother. She eventually regained consciousness with a humongous headache. The doctor advised her to get some rest for the next couple of days.

As for my grandfather, the doctor said it was a good thing that my grandmother was able to slow down the bleeding or else my grandfather would have bled to death before reaching his office.

He was rushed to the nearest hospital where he spent four days before being released from the hospital. My grandmother took the doctor's advice. She relaxed for a couple of days to recover from the ordeal.

My dad was able to stop the hiccups. He would move his hands back and forth in front of the person's chest that was suffering from a bad case of hiccups. He would do like a scooping motion with his hands and say *I got it*. The person's hiccup was gone.

My dad would tease my mom if he passed before my mom.

"If I go before you, I will come back and tickle your toes."

"Thank you for telling me. If my toes are being tickled, I will know it's you."

A few months before my dad passed away, every morning, he would say to my mom.

"Sit on the side of the bed with me for a few minutes. I do not have too much time left. My days are numbered."

"Stop talking like that. You know I do not like it when you say that."

"It`s a feeling that I have. I want you to be prepared when the time comes."

I knew he was right. I never told my mom. A month or so after telling my mom that his days were numbered, he was admitted to the hospital for a bladder infection. My dad said to my mom,

"I am not going to leave this place."

"Do not talk that way. You know I get very nervous when you say things like that. You will be home in no time. "

Again I knew my dad was right. When my dad was admitted to the hospital, there was an epidemic spreading like wildfire in the hospitals. The virus found its way to my dad`s room. He was transferred to a ward for infectious diseases. Before entering his room, we needed to wear a mask-- a special garment.

The doctor prepared my mom for the unavoidable.

"Your husband only has a few days to live. "

He died three days later.

I was by his bedside all night which happened to be his final night. In the morning, my mom and sister arrived to spend the day with my dad. My dad`s watch was on a table beside his bed. I noticed the needle for the seconds started to move, the watch started working.

The watch needed a new battery. I was intrigued as to why the watch would start working. I then realized the watch was counting down the time before my dad would pass away. That morning before leaving the hospital, I shook my dad's hand. In a very weak voice he said,

"Thank you."

"I will see you tonight."

He shook his head.

"No."

I shook my head in a yes motion, went home to get some sleep. I was convinced that my dad would still be with us for a few more days. I was wrong. Like I said, the visions that I see can change, that's what happened with my dad. I was in bed for about an hour when my sister called.

"If you want to see dad one more time before he goes, you will have to hurry."

The hospital was thirty minutes away. My dad passed away while I was on my way to the hospital. When I entered the room, my dad looked at peace. I glanced at my dad's watch on the table, it was again idle.

From the time I noticed the time on the watch, and the time until the watch stopped functioning again; the watch functioned for two and a half hours. The same period of time when I went home and back to the hospital.

That morning when I went home, two of my cousins Joanne and Pauline who were very close to my mom and dad arrived at the hospital. They went directly to my dad's room. Both were still at the hospital along with my two brothers who arrived a few minutes before me. When my cousins spotted me in the hallway, one of my cousins walked over to me.

"You missed seeing your dad alive for the last time by five minutes. Anyway, when we arrived we told your mom and sister to go to the cafeteria and grab some breakfast. We still have goosebumps just by telling you what we witnessed in the final moments before your dad passed away."

"What did you see?"

"A few minutes before your mom and sister came back from breakfast, your dad was agitated and looking up at the ceiling; his finger was signaling at something or someone to give him a minute."

"Were you able to see who my dad was signaling?"

"No, he was also fighting to free himself from whatever or whoever had a hold of him. When your mom and sister entered the room, we said to your mom that he was waiting for them."

"He was combatant."

"Yes, he was, so your sister went over the other side of the bed. She put her hand in your dad's hand, your mom did the same on the other side of the bed. He calmed down, took two big breath, and he was gone."

My cousins were completely freaked out at what they witnessed. We all said our final goodbye and they took my dad away. That was the last time that I was able to see my dad's face except in photos. When I arrived home, I went to bed. When I entered the bedroom, I noticed my dad's picture on a book that was on my dresser.

The book was moved from one dresser to another, it was my dad's way to let me know that he was gone. Ironically, my dad's funeral was on the same day as my son's birthday. For a short period of time, at night my mom would hear my dad with his walker in the hallway making his way to their bedroom.

When dreaming spirits can send you messages. I know by experience. My mom had a dream that my dad was sitting on his coffin and said when the time comes, I will be right here waiting for you.

My uncle-- the husband of one of my mom's sisters, passed away from cancer. A few days before he died, my aunt was at his bedside. She noticed that my uncle was staring at the empty chair in the corner of the room.

"It won't be long before I go and join you."

My aunt replied ,

"Who are you talking to?"

"My brother, he is sitting in the chair."

"There's nobody in the chair so how can you be talking to your brother who passed away several years ago?"

"I am telling you, he is waiting for me to join him."

My uncle passed away the following afternoon.

My best friend's brother was dying of aids, results of sharing a needle for building muscle. A few days before he died, his sister walked into his hospital room.

Her brother was sitting at the foot of the bed having a conversation with someone she could not see. He was talking a language she did not understand.

"Who are you talking to?"

"I am talking to Jesus."

"You are talking to Jesus really, in what language?"

"The Hebrew language."

"You're talking to Jesus in Hebrew."

"Yes, the Hebrew language. I guess my conversation with Jesus is over, he is walking away. Strange, while having my discussion with Jesus, I could talk Hebrew as if I mastered the language years ago and now I cannot remember one word in Hebrew. Strange is it?"

"It sure is strange. Were you really talking to Jesus. It's not a side effect of your medication that makes you hear and see things?"

"Yes, I was talking to Jesus it was not an illusion or side effects either. I am taking the same medication for the past month and I never suffered any side effects. He told me to be prepared because it won't be long before I join him in heaven."

The following day, on her way to the hospital to visit her brother; she was listening to the radio-- one of her favorite songs came on. When she entered the room, she sat in a chair near her brother's bed. She was still thinking about the song.

"Good morning, I really like that song."

"What song?"

"The song that you are playing over and over in your head."

She was dumbfounded.

"How can you know which song I keep replaying in my head.?"

"I have no clue, I just know ."

What they did not know was they both experienced 'telepathy'.

"You were never able to read minds before."

"I know. For some reason, I know the song that you have in your head. One thing that I forgot to mention, yesterday, when I talked to Jesus he mentioned to make sure everything was in order. In a few days I will be in heaven."

"I know, you mentioned it yesterday."

"Sorry, I have no recollection of mentioning it."

"That's okay."

He passed away the following evening. He was only thirty years old.

When my elderly neighbor passed away, I could see her spirit going in and out of her house. She was checking on her son that was living with her when she passed away.

Chapter 7

The public is driving me nuts wanting to know, how do I know when a spirit needs guidance and what do I see. It's a feeling that I get when the spirit/soul is on his way to see me; I go into a trance, I see a full body apparition for about five seconds then I see a white light, the size of a golf ball that expands when a spirit comes through .

I am alongside the spirit until it reaches heaven. The spirit goes through another white light that expands the size of a baseball and when the white light shuts off, the spirit is in heaven.

I can tell when a spirit is going straight to hell. First of all there is no white light. They make their way in a funnel where the black entities grab them and whisk them away to their new home for eternity. I do not get involved; it would complicate things. They are going to hell for some reason or another. Some spirits I cannot guide, they refuse to cross over.

They go their own way to find whatever they are looking for. Some are afraid of the beyond, the unknown after dying. They can remain in limbo for years and years.

Sometimes I wonder how people think asking me bizarre questions such as if I always carry a kit that contains sulfur, salt, holy water, sage, a cross, the whole nine yards. They also want information if I know where to purchase those items. My response is always the same.

"Go see a priest, maybe he will be able to give you some information if there is such a kit."

Also questions like-- *do you think the priest would be willing to give me holy water? Do you think it depends on the circumstances? Do you know if there is a demand for holy water? Is there a charge if he provides me with holy water?*

"How the heck am I supposed to know that stuff? Talk to a priest, not me."

Another question, the public keeps pestering me with my assistance… *would they be able to communicate with their loved ones that passed away?* I answer.

"Go see a psychic".

Some responded; they will not go see a psychic ,they charge a fee.

"So you think it's okay to bother me for free. What makes you think that it would be free? The more I get irritated, the more my fee goes up."

That usually puts an end to the annoying questions. Inquiries-- if I can perform an exorcism. Same answer, to go see a priest. Is there a fee to go see the priest? The most frequent question is, if i am a paranormal investigator.

I wish people would listen and pay attention when you talk to them. Wishful thinking on my part. You address thirty people in a room. When you are done talking then ask if everything that was said is clear. Does everybody understand? You will get thirty different versions, solutions, opinions and answers.

It is said and proven by research when you address the public, only ten percent will listen; that's why ninety percent of the gossip is always wrong and exaggerated. Word of mouth everybody will always insert a few extra words in the story until it balloons out of proportion.

Some individuals are afraid that I will reveal their secrets. I let them know *how could I reveal your secrets, I cannot read minds*. I advise them it's none of my business with what you do with your lives. I have my own problems to deal with. They assumed that I could read minds. For example, one guy came up to me.

"I know you can read minds. If you know what is good for you, keep your mouth shut."

I started laughing.

"First of all, I do not read minds. Who told you I could read minds, or you assumed I could read minds? Another thing, you cannot approach someone with threats; they will be on the defensive to protect themselves."

He replied,

"It's a simple warning."

"I wish I could read minds when a nut like you is coming towards me, I would be prepared to deal with what the nut case wants from me before he reaches me and waste my time."

He was looking at me with nothing to say.

"I have a question for you. Why act like a bully? If you are trying to intimidate me with your words. I have news for you, I do not get intimidated by anyone especially an asshole like you."

"Are you calling me an asshole?"

"Yes, I did and what made you think that I would poke my nose in your personal life? What you do in life it is your own business. What would be in it for me? Can you answer my question?"

A long pause.

"Just as I thought you have no answers. If I could read minds I would not be able to read yours. You cannot read a mind when there is nothing to read. Yours is probably like a book with only blank pages."

For a lot of people, I am a weirdo. I tell them to stay away from me to leave me alone or else I will put a curse on each one of you. It's a good thing they do not know that I am not able to put a curse on anyone.

I cannot go out anywhere. When people spot me, they run to me for information. Some are just curious, some intrigued, some non-believers. Healthy people want to know how long will they live.

I am getting really tired of always repeating the same old, same old thing. I do not know when my time will come. I get a lot of letters of course; some are sarcastic. After reading a few words, the letters are in the recycle bin.

Some letters from individuals that are too shy to come talk to me, they do not know how to approach me when they need help or information. I reply to those letters as soon as possible.

Some might not like the response to their letter. People know that I tell it like it is. I do not play games. I never reply with false information or sugar coat the answers. I ran into a person that I have known for years but not really a friend. First words out of his mouth…

"Are you still a freak and talking to the dead? Do you still claim that you have special powers?"

I ignored him not worth wasting my saliva answering his questions. Sometimes, I rather deal with an angry spirit instead of people.

I was thinking to go see a psychic, see what she or he had to say. Curiosity got the best of me. I decided to go see one and see what she or he had to say.

My niece who blocked her psychic abilities when she was a kid was curious what the psychic would tell me so she tagged along. She declined to talk to the psychic. While waiting for me, she was able to see spirits roaming in the building.

The first thing the lady told me that I was an indigo child, I have to admit she was good. She divulged a lot of information that only myself knew about the things she told me.

She advised me to be careful concerning my heart and to go see a doctor. It's a good thing that I took her advice. My cholesterol level was way too high, my blood pressure was also too high. The psychic also mentioned not to worry about my kids, they will be around for a very long time. Ironic, I have a boy and a girl.

"How many kids do you have?"

"Two-- a boy and a girl."

She also mentioned my niece's medical problems. She also predicted a breakup regarding a sibling. A few months after her prediction, my niece and her boyfriend ended their relationship.

"Your dad just came through. Did you win an award?"

"Yes, a few months ago. The provincial government gave me an award for my longevity with the fire department."

"Your dad was there, he is very proud of you."

She also mentioned that my wife was going on a trip. Everything will be okay, no mishaps. She also hit the nail on the head with that prediction, my wife was going on a cruise with her aunt, her sister and a close friend.

I said to myself.

"So far so good, she is good."

"Who are the soldiers? They are both dressed in a civil war uniform."

"Funny that you would talk about a war. I was once hypnotized. Apparently, I was a sniper for the British army in the second world war. I was killed four days after D-day. I took a bullet to the throat."

I paused for a moment.

"I don' t know if it's a coincidence or not. When I try to pronounce certain words, I stutter. As per shooting a rifle without any practice, I always hit the bullseye."

"It looks like you come from a family that was involved in the civil war and both world wars."

"My grandfather's dad was wounded while fighting in the first world war. I am always fascinated by war."

"Who is the hunter holding two partridges?"

"That must be my dear friend who departed way too quick from this earth. We used to go hunting together."

She warned me to be very careful to be on the lookout for mishaps, bad luck. She mentioned.

"Your grandmother, your mom's mom is always by your side. Archangel Micheal is never far away if you need him, because from what I see you will need all the help you can get."

"Yes, I know. Sometimes, I feel like calling the armed forces for help."

There are three black entities around you. One more just showed up. He is indicating that the worse is yet to come. They will keep haunting you because of what you do."

"It's not easy being an indigo child."

"I can well imagine that it's no walk in the park. "

When I was about to leave, she said.

"Remember what I told you-- be careful."

She was right the worst was yet to come.

Chapter 8

One thing that I do know if I help someone or do a good deed which disrupts the entities intentions, I know they will not be happy with me, and they will pay me a visit. One night, while in bed, a black shadow shaped like a demon bit my fingers then vanished. He bit my fingers hard enough to make two of my fingers bleed. I wonder if that demon loves finger food.

Later that same night, my face was smashed in my pillow; I was unable to breathe. My wife woke up and saw the black shadow on the side of the bed, holding my head on my pillow. When she looked at him, he vanished. It took a minute or two for me to be able to catch my breath. I wonder what would have been the outcome if my wife would have not woken up?

One night, I was on my way to the grocery store, three black shadows were coming along for the ride. Two in the back seat and one in the front passenger seat. All three were looking at me.

I stopped on the side of the road. I started to pray as loud as I could, without damaging my lungs. I made sure all three were able to see the cross around my neck that was dipped in holy water and also blessed by a priest.

They vanished. That cross never leaves my neck. On occasions, the entities really get to me. I get very angry but not for long. I get a calm, relaxing feeling that brings me back to earth. Again, I went to see Father Joseph. I wanted to know who was helping me to calm down after an episode with entities that are a real pain in the butt.

"Your guardian angel helps you calm down before you do something foolish that you may regret. You need to keep your cool, you know they will keep taunting you in hopes that you will give in and walk away."

"We both know that I am not a quitter."

"I can appreciate that but be careful we all have our breaking points."

"I will do my best to not let them get under my skin. Sometimes, it's easier said than done."

"Make sure to stay in touch. As long as you have your cross around your neck, you will be safe. No harm will come to you."

I truly believed, the cross will always keep me out of danger; until one incident that put a lot of doubt in my mind when it comes to my safety with the cross around my neck. That day I came home, as soon as I opened the door an entity was waiting for me, I was pushed down the basement stairs.

When you enter my home from the backdoor that leads to the kitchen, you are facing the basement stairs so a good shove can make you tumble until you hit the basement floor. We always keep the basement door closed so as not to fall down the stairs. We close the door and after a few minutes, the door opens by itself.

I should say the door opens with the help of a black spirit. The entity stood there, looked at me, let out a scream that still send shivers down my spine just talking about it. He exited the premises through the door. To this day, I still remember what he looked like.

A solid entity shaped somewhat like a human being with short legs that looked like legs from a goat, hands with extra long fingers, a face that I have a hard time describing, red eyes, no ears, a very scary face like I said, is very hard to describe.

In my entire life, I have never seen such an ugly face. I have friends that are ugly, but the entity takes the cake. No cheeks, no ears, small mouth. A distorted look in his eyes; even his color was hard to describe, it looked almost like a charcoal mossy color. I have not seen that entity since that day.

When I discussed the incident with Father Joseph, he was surprised that my cross did not protect me from harm.

"The only thing that I can think of it was the devil himself that pushed you down the stairs. I was sure the cross would be powerful enough to keep the devil a safe distance from you. I underestimated him. He is more powerful since the last time I had to deal with him."

"You mean to tell me he is getting more powerful."

"Years ago, a young man came to see me after moving in a house near the cemetery. Every night, he was attacked by an entity. I gave the young man some holy water, a cross that was blessed by me and dipped in holy water.

"The tools you gave him helped to get rid of the entity."

"That's right. I also told him to pray out loud when the entity would make his appearance. The young man told me after several nights of throwing holy water in his direction, praying out loud with the cross in his hands; the entity decided not to come back."

The priest gave me a bottle of holy water.

"Keep the bottle close at hand. If for some reason you need to use the holy water; if you notice that the bottle is almost empty... come see me for a refill. No serious injuries, I hope. When were you pushed?"

"No, I was halfway down the stairs. I was able to grab a hold of the railing. A few bumps, bruises, a bleeding elbow... nothing serious. Do you think that was a warning, or a message of some kind?"

"The push down the stair... his purpose was to hurt you. Stay alert and be careful, they will keep on trying to hurt you."

When I drove home, I could see feathers in the driveway. A message from one of my elders wanted me to contact him. When I contacted my elder, he had this to say.

"The entity that pushed you down the stairs was not the devil but one of his disciples. He was sent to hurt you, to cause you a lot of pain, so you would back off and not help or guide the spirits that come see you. They want to lure every spirit to hell. Be very careful."

"One of his disciples?"

"Yes, one of his disciples."

"I was not aware that the devil had disciples."

"Now you know. I am certain another of the devil's disciples will strike again when you least expect it. They have you in their sights. They are out to maim you or worse… if you know what I mean."

"I do, I will be very diligent and cautious. I will try not to let my guard down. I am curious on how did you find out about me being pushed down the stairs?"

"We held a ceremony in the native circle and we were able to see you pushed down the stair by a grey entity. We will also try to keep you safe."

The pushing down the stairs incident… everything that was said, warnings really made me think; wonder if I should keep going or call it quits. I started to doubt myself, then it occurred to me. This is precisely what the entities want. Their goal is for me to be confused, worried what might come next.

I went and found a quiet place for a few days to clear my head-- to reflect on the consequences it might bring if I keep pushing forward. I convinced myself that I need to keep my head high and not let the entities get the best of me.

I now have a pretty good idea what to expect; be better prepared. With the help of my elders and the help of Father Joseph, I should be okay. I constantly need to remind myself that I am not a quitter.

The house was quiet for several weeks, until my wife saw a black mass shaped like a human with red eyes. He was standing in the hallway. He warned my wife to *get ready, they need souls…* then vanished.

I now see more and more black shadows--double the amount that I used to see. I think their plan of attack is to keep me wondering or nervous as to when they will strike again.

I see them everywhere-- they glance at me and disappear. With my wife being a sensitive person, she can hear, see spirits but unable to convey or have a conversation with the entities. She sees a lot of entities in the house.

We have things disappear or moved to different places in the house. We search for the items thinking they were just misplaced. We are unable to locate the items anywhere in the house. Some items we found, they were moved to another part of the house. A critic poked his nose where it does not belong.

"An individual was in my house and stole the items."

Which is not the case. I told him that he was wrong and did not know what he was talking about.

"What gives you the right to poke your nose in my business? Who died and made you a king?"

He shrugged his shoulders and walked away.

That night we go to bed. The next morning, items on the night table are missing and were never seen again. Where the items end up or who took them… I have no idea. We know that neither one of us took the items and we are the only ones living in the house. Maybe it's a way for the entities to let me know that they are always close watching us or they are stealing stuff to have a yard sale.

That is why I am not too crazy about sleeping. First of all, I always said sleep is a waste of time, I feel vulnerable. You take for example, you live until you're sixty. You sleep eight hours a day, that means you were catching zzz for a third of your life. Twenty years of sleep, if there was no need to sleep to recharge our batteries, we would have all that extra time on our hands to do other things.

One of the methods of communication that the spirits/ souls/ archangels use to contact me, warn me of imminent danger; they use the lights to send messages. It can be any kind of light-- street lights, parked car lights, front porch lights, indoor lights.

If a light blinks a couple of times, it means to be careful because there is trouble ahead. If it's an encounter with a dark shadow, hang on to your hat you might be in for a rough ride. If a light is on and turns off, that means the grim reaper has claimed another victim. If a light comes on, it means a new message or event is on the horizon.

One night when I came home I had to deal with black entities. One was floating close to the ceiling, the other one was standing in the kitchen-- pointed a very long, narrow finger at me. I shouted.

"Get out of my house, you have no right to be here. You were not invited, you are trespassing on a private property." The entity that was floating close to the ceiling joined the other entity that was standing in the kitchen. They were both looking at me. I stood my ground I again yelled.

"Get out of my house!"

All the lights in the house turned off at the same time, complete darkness. I could not see a thing, one entity came very close to me a few inches from my face. His eyes were green. He let out a growl. I could feel heat on my stomach. The other entity grabbed my hair, slammed my head on the wall.

The lights came back on, they were both gone. My stomach was red and yellow... a bruise the size of a quarter. A small bump on the back of my head. When my wife came home, I filled her in on my ordeal. My wife shook her head. She took a look at my stomach and the back of my head. I reassured her that I was alright.

Once in a while, I need a break-- disappear, escape for a week of fishing, hunting with friends. Hopefully, a week without having to deal with the pesky nimrods causing me grief. It never works; they always find me. I wonder if they use a tracking device maybe a GPS to track me down, there is no escape. I bought a waterfront cottage so that I could go relax, do a little bit of fishing, but no luck.

The couple who owns one of the neighboring cottages-- the lady who battled cancer. As soon as she noticed I was at my cottage. She would come over to ask a ton of questions. I feel for her. I really did, in a way I don't blame her, she was in remission. She wanted to know if her cancer would come back. Also, a bunch of questions I could not answer.

They were good neighbors but there is a limit, you need to draw the line somewhere. I was also visited by spirits. I eventually sold the cottage. The purchase of the cottage was not doing its purpose. I was not getting any peace and quiet-- the main reason for purchasing the cottage in the first place.

I have to admit some mornings were nice and quiet, but not for long. At night, during a full moon, there was a nice reflection on the lake. You could hear the loons which was nice, but it was not worth the money that I was spending to upkeep the place. I sold it at a loss. Well nothing ventured, nothing gained.

I will never forget the day that I was approached in a parking lot by a devil worshipper. The first words came out of his mouth.

"What you are doing is not right. Spirits should choose themselves where they want to go."

"Excuse me, do I know you?"

"No."

"What you just said does not make any sense. You don't know what you are talking about. The spirits come to see me on their own accord. You should know all souls want to go to heaven. I agree some should go to hell."

"Not all the souls want to go to heaven."

"Let me get this straight, your telling me that not every soul wants to go to heaven. What comic book did you read to give that assumption? I guess I am not talking to someone who wants to go to heaven."

"That's none your business if I want to go to heaven or not."

"Listen, I am not a judge to tell them where they should go. I only guide them. If you need to know, the souls come to me to help them to get into god's house."

"Not all the spirits come to see you."

"As I was saying, it is god's decision if he will let the soul enter in heaven. It depends on the sins, the individual committed while being alive."

"Why does he have a court of law up there?"

"Do you know that we are all born innocent and we all die guilty of something. I cannot deny that. Who do you think you are, coming at me with such a tone in your voice and say what I do is not right?"

"I am a member of a cult that worships the true messiah-- the devil himself."

"Really."

"Yes, indeed. We meet once a month at a secret location not too far from here. Our members are all from the area-- some from your town. You never know it could be one of your neighbors.

"I couldn't care less who your members are."

"We have a meeting coming up next week, come join us take an oath of allegiance and secrecy to the most powerful king in the world. You will be amazed at the rituals we do."

"I don't think so, you are barking up the wrong tree. Are you a recruiter for this so-called cult?"

"We would love for you to join us."

"Have you lost your mind? You're crazy if you think that I will join a group of deranged, twisted individuals released from a mental institution? Leave me alone. How come you know my name? I do not know who you are."

"People talk my friend."

"I am not your friend. Do you have any brothers and sisters?"

"Only one sister."

"Your mom did not raise too many stupid kids; there are only two of you. I know one of your family member shook your family tree and nuts fell off the branches, and I am talking to one right now. I don't have time for this nonsense."

"I have not spoken to my parents and sister in years."

"I wonder why?"

I opened my car door to leave. He grabbed the door.

"You are making a big mistake. Come on, get with the program and join us. You are alone in your quest. We are a large group. You could see the devil. Look him in the eye."

"First of all, I am not on a quest and you would be surprised how many followers that I have. Why don't you do everyone a favor? Put your lips over your head and swallow. Your mouth would be in a perfect position to kiss your own ass."

"Are you trying to be funny?"

"I don't need to be funny; I am talking to a bozo. Now let go of my car door and get lost. Did you really think that you were going to hit a home run by convincing me to join your cult? Tell your so called leader and all of you to kiss my ass including you."

"I am going to disregard your comments."

"A word of advice before having a conversation with someone-- take something for your breath. I do not know how many butts you kissed today but do something about your breath; it almost made me vomit."

"Stop insulting me. I don't call you names."

"If I would have known in advance that I would be talking to you, I would have brought a barf bag with me. Here is a few bucks, go buy yourself some *tic tacs*. I hope that you are not the main speaker at your gatherings of idiots, everyone would be puking."

"Enough with the insults."

"It just occurred to me that you must be eating shit on a daily basis to be able to tell me the load of crap that you just told me. That's the reason for your polluting stench that comes out of the hole in your face. Leave me alone, you moron."

"We are going to put a curse on you."

"Go ahead, asswipe!"

"You and your wife."

"Leave her alone. She does not have anything to do with this dumb conversation. Let me educate you, I am a calm individual. Right now, you are pressing too many buttons."

"Yah Yah Yah."

"When I get mad, I am a totally different person. It's something that you do not want to see. I would say, like the green hulk… don't make me angry you won't like me when I am angry."

"Green hulk… what are you talking about?"

"Keep on holding my car door and you will be the recipient of my anger. Do you know or brainwashed to know that you and your messiah followers will never be able to go to heaven?"

"We don't care if we do not go to heaven."

"You will all rot in hell. Your grand poobah does not care about you guys, you are pawns for him. Like a fisherman who threw a line, all of you swallowed the bait, hook, line and sinker, when he is done with all of you."

"Okay, okay. I get the message."

"He will collect your souls and never set them free."

"I dont think so."

"Do you think so or you know so? Just watch and see. I have had enough go back to your group of the devil's slaves. Don't forget to tell them they are welcomed to kiss my ever expanding butt."

That was several years ago, I have not heard or seen him since that day. Maybe his powerful messiah made a human sacrifice out of him and if they did put a curse on me… which I believe they did not, I would have noticed.

Chapter 9

With my career as a firefighter, first responder, I have seen things that no human being should see. I won't go into details, some are too gory to describe. One particular call, something very strange happened to me.

We get a 911 call. The address that we were responding to was the address of a very close friend. He and his wife were both killed in a car accident, leaving behind five young daughters aged between eleven months and 11 years old.

My friend's sister along with her husband decided to move in to take care of the girls so that they could stay at home and be able to stay together. One year, the whole family went on vacation during March break.

While they were on vacation, their son-inlaw would go check on the house. The house was heated with electric baseboard heaters and an airtight wood furnace located in the basement.

Before going home, he would go in the basement to put some firewood in the furnace. The house was equipped with an alarm system connected to a central station.

The 911 dispatcher advised us that the smoke detectors where activated, and nobody was answering the home phone. When we arrived at the scene, their son inlaw lives only a few houses down the street and when he saw the fire trucks, he came running and unlocked the door.

I was the first firefighter to enter the house. When I entered the house, I was overwhelmed with a sensation that my deceased friend took over my body. The way, I was talking as if I was the owner of the house. I told the guys to make sure that everything was safe and secured before we leave.

My fellow firefighters were looking at me with a puzzled look on their faces. Then the"all clear" was given. While walking out of the house, he released me. I was myself again. Some of my brothers in crime wanted to know what was that all about. Not to start a debate or argument, I replied

"I have no idea."

One of my fellow comrades interjected.

"You have no idea."

"That's right, I have no idea. End of story."

So again, I went to see Father Joseph. I explained the whole thing to him. His first question.

"Was there a lot of damage to the house?"

"No."

"Thank God. The poor girls have been through enough already. Will they be able to stay in the house when they get back from vacation?"

"Yes, they will be able to stay at home when they come back. Only a bit of smoke damage."

"What caused the problem?"

"Before leaving to go home, their son-inlaw closed the main draft of the wood furnace by mistake. The smoke did not have anywhere to go but in the house. Relatives will do a thorough cleanup of the house before the family comes back from vacation."

"Good for them. Now back to your original question, your friend took over your body because he trusted you and you would make sure that everything was okay with the house before leaving."

"Like we always do, we never leave a scene before the"all clear" is given. It's mandatory."

"He wanted a firsthand look of what was going on. You see, we have the proof that deceased family members can watch over their loved ones from heaven."

"Trust me, Father. I do not need any proof with everything that I have seen so far; I would be a fool not to believe, that was one heck of a feeling."

"How are you coping with all of this?"

"I am doing fine, thank you for asking. Father, there is a question that I have been meaning to ask you. How do they know to come see me?"

"The spirits?"

"Yes."

"Don't tell me you are beginning to forget our discussions. You know the answer to your question. They just know, they are drawn to you."

"Sorry, I am confused on how fast my friend was able to take over my body. Funny how things work, I will say it again, *god works in mysterious ways*. The only thing that I still do not approve was the way god worked, to get me to believe and what needed to be done."

"Still moping about the event. And yes, god sure does work in mysterious ways that will never change."

"Thank you again for your patience."

"You're quite welcomed. Until next time."

"Yes sir."

When we are dispatched for a house fire-- accident which involves possible fatalities, I need to concentrate a lot more than my comrades on what I am doing. I will see what other people cannot see.

One accident scene, the driver of a car involved in the accident. He was badly injured and succumbed from his wounds a few minutes before the ambulance arrived. I was able to observe the victim's spirit leave his body. He was standing close to where he was laying on the pavement, watching the paramedics trying to revive him.

He looked towards the sky and then looked at me, nodded his head in the yes motion then floated towards the clouds. When we get back to the fire station, a debriefing is mandatory. I never talk about what I see and what the other first responders were not able to see.

Over the years, I have noticed when I am providing first aid to an injured patient, they never take their eyes off me. They follow my every move. They can sense something about me. They want me to get in the ambulance with them. I always reassure the patients that they are in good hands.

I always do my best to keep them alive, knowing some will not make it, at least I give them a fighting chance. I try not to show any emotions, keep a straight face… but it's not easy. When the ambulance leaves the scene, I always hope that I could be wrong. Unfortunately, it's never the case.

Every call is confidential. Like I previously stated, a debriefing and a written report are mandatory. We keep a copy of the report. A copy is also sent to the fire marshall, or police department in case there was a wrongdoing by someone.

The public keeps pestering me for details about the victim. Will he or she make it?

"We are asking you because we know that you know."

I keep repeating again over and over."You guys know that I cannot answer any of your questions so why bother. Leave me alone so that I can have some peace and quiet."

One night, we were battling an out-of-control fire of a very large house. When we were finally able to bring the fire under control, my partner and I went down in the basement to tackle the fire from a different angle.

The floor above our heads was made of cement, the floor kept us safe from any falling debris. When it came the time to exit the basement, while going up the stairs, I tripped and fell backwards with the breathing apparatus on my back.

I landed between the basement wall and the stairs. I was jammed, unable to move. What a predicament I got myself in. My partner radioed for help before they were able to get me out of there.

I had to remove my mask to be able to breathe my breathing apparatus was empty. The flames were about six feet from me. The basement entrance was made of lumber; it did not take long before the flames found their way towards me.

I thought my time was up. I was about to meet my maker. I started to pray, thinking of my kids. I felt a pair of hands touching my back, it was not the hands of any of the guys who were working to get me out of there.

I was convinced it was the hands of an angel-- my grandmother; my mom's mom helping to get me to safety. With the combination of immense pain, inhaled smoke, I passed out. I remember opening my eyes a few times in the ambulance .

Once in the hospital's emergency room, they placed me on a bed on my stomach. The doctor gave me a needle of morphine. I went for x-rays and brought back to my bed.

With the combination of painkillers and fatigue, I fell asleep. The following morning, I was still on my stomach. Again, I could feel a pair of hands touching my back. I was alone in my room.

"Who is in the room with me?"

I saw a light. It was my grandmother smiling at me. We were always very close; there she was from the afterlife looking out for me. The psychic mentioned that my grandmother was always by my side.

The psychic predicted that I will have back problems due to an injury. I spent twenty-two days in the hospital before going home. While in the hospital, a lot of people came to visit me.

Skeptic and non-believers kept telling me the reason I saw my grandmother is-- it was the side effects of the medication the doctor was giving me to ease the pain.

One of my fellow first responders and a very close friend came to visit a few times. His first visit he said.

"I have something to tell you that might sound strange to you. While we were working to get you out of the basement, I could see a small round light floating over you."

"So you did see the light"

"I do not know if some of the guys were also able to see the light or if they did, they are keeping it to themselves. This is the first time that I have talked to someone about it."

"It was not strange at all. It was my grandmother."

"How do you know that?"

"Well, like you said, the guys were doing their best to get me out of there ASAP. I could feel an extra pair of hands."

"Really."

"The morning after my accident, I again felt the same pair of hands touching my back. I was able to see my grandmother in the same little ball of light that you saw."

"That explains a lot of things. I should know by now, we might see strange things happening around you."

"How is your dad?"

"Feeling a lot better, thanks for asking. Well, I have to go. Get better soon. We miss you at the station."

When I told my mom about the light, she smiled.

"I am not surprised. You were always her first and favorite grandson."

To this day, I am still plagued with back pain. A short time after my accident, my sister suffered a massive heart attack and did not survive. Fourteen months later, my mom passed away; and my dad who passed away a few years before my sister. I lost three family members in a span of four years.

Seven months later, our family came close to suffer another casualty. My niece, the daughter of my dear departed sister was gravely ill. She managed to pull through and thank god she is still with us.

I also went through a very difficult divorce, mayhem with the spirits, emergency calls with the fire department. I was worried that my brain would explode-- it took a mental toll on me. I was starting to question my sanity.

When my sister passed away, I was at work. I did not have a chance to say goodbye. My mom passed away at the hospital, my brother and I, we were both by my mom's bedside. A few moments before my mom passed away, both our chairs jolted.

We looked at each other. I put my hand on my mom's chest. She took a final breath. When our chairs jolted, she was sending us a message. She was leaving us, going to heaven to join my dad and my sister. I never took my eyes off her spirit while it was making its way to heaven.

With all the events that was happening, I continued to be plagued with the paranormal. One evening, I was cleaning the basement. I almost jumped out of my shoes because of a loud bang on a can no more than three feet away from me."

"Who are you? What do you want? Show yourself."

Nothing but the sound of silence. My wife ran downstairs.

"What was that noise?"

"A big bang on the can in front of you, and it was not me."

"Will that nonsense ever stop?"

"Your guess is as good as mine, honey."

My wife was shaking her head as she went back upstairs.

One night, a powerful thunderstorm passed through our region, which caused a power outage. When the outage was over, all the lights (electricity) were restored. The power was back on except for my house.

I went to my neighbor's house to call the power company, they checked the grid, they could not find anything wrong, I should have power. I thanked my neighbor for the use of the phone, I walked back home.

As soon as I walked in the house, the entities blew out all the candles in the house. I was in the dark; I could not see a thing. I was shoved, pushed, scratched, and punched in the gut. The beating lasted for about maybe two or three minutes. When they were done, the lights came back on.

I had scratches on my neck, my back, and bruises in my face and stomach. My wife was in the living room and came running to see if I was alright.

"Yes, I am okay. A few bruises and nothing to worry about."

"Easy for you to say not to worry."

"Let's put this behind us and go watch T.V."

"Honey, we need to do something ."

I did not let her finish what she had to say.

"Like I said, let's put this behind us."

"but, honey…"

"What did I just say?"

"Okay, okay. I am sorry to be concerned and worried about you. I am going to bed."

Early one morning, we were sound asleep. A big bang from under the bed woke us up followed by a big bang in the kitchen. I ran to the kitchen, everything was where it should be. The following day, I saw a black shadow in the house. We locked eyes for a few seconds, and he disappeared.

It's a never-ending game they enjoy playing at my expense. Again, another chat with Father Joseph.

"The reason they make their moves in the dark, they know you cannot see them; so they can inflict more pain. They changed their strategies."

"I know. I got a taste of their new tactics."

"They are aware that in the dark, your cross is useless; the same for every weapon in your arsenal because you cannot see them."

"They are sneaky. I can tell you that much."

"Yes, they are clever. They know in the dark, you cannot locate the necessary tools to do battle. Also, you cannot fight what you do not see."

I decided to make another appointment with the same psychic of several years ago and see if she would be able to give me some insight on what to expect in the near future. The first thing she said since my last visit, my sister and my mother passed away. We were talking about my sister.

"Your sister just came through. She is indicating to me that she misses you and you two were very close."

"Yes, we were."

"She is also telling me that she is okay and she is with a brother and a dog."

"Wait a minute, how can she be with a brother. Both my brothers are still alive?"

"The first time you were here, you mentioned that your mom had two miscarriages-- one was early in her pregnancy, the second miscarriage was one month away from her due date. It's the spirit of your unborn brother. A white dog is by her side."

"The white dog was a large husky. It was her dog and was by her side for many years.

"Your sister is leaving, waving goodbye. Another lady has joined us, she is showing me the letter c."

"My mom's name starts with the letter c."

"Your mom is showing me her legs. Did she have a problem with her legs?"

"Yes."

"She is also indicating that she did not want to go but she could no longer take the pain. Your dad has joined us. He says that he always keeps an eye on you and your family. They are waving goodbye. They are both gone."

The psychic also mentioned not to worry about December 2012, the world will not end. We will all be here in 2013. We talked about my kids. She said not to worry. They are doing well and they will keep doing well for a very long time. We discussed my wife's health.

"Her well-being will improve and she will be able to return to her daily routines; but you my friend, all I see is negativity, black orbs around you. They say, if you give in, they will leave you alone."

"That remains to be seen that if they would leave me alone, they cannot be trusted."

Just then soft music started to play. I looked at her.

"It's not me, the music came on by itself. This is first for me that the music came on by itself. Amazing. So anyway, I now see angels by your side."

"Yes, always by my side when I do not need them; and when I do need them, they are nowhere to be seen."

"They are indicating. They will try to keep a wall of protection around you but it's not always easy. The black entities are very powerful."

"The entities will have a battle on their hands for a very long time to come. I will not give in, I will not let them win."

"Be diligent and careful, I can see a lot of darkness. You better keep your eyes on the ball, my friend. I see band aids and injuries. I know that you are a first responder but what I see does not relate to your job. The visions that I see are aimed at you."

When the session was over, I thanked her.

"Again, you are amazing on how accurate you were on everything we talked about."

"Well, thank you. You know where to find me."

That same night, we were getting ready for bed. My wife heard a growl a few feet from her. I threw some holy water in that direction and shouted.

"Get lost."

The entity let out a gut-wrenching growl. After the growl, everything was quiet. Some holy water must have landed on him. One night, I was dreaming that I was at war against evil forces. When I woke up, my wife told me that *I was talking three different languages that she never heard before.*

The thing is, I do not remember talking three languages in my dream. One day when I came home, my wife told me that: Earlier in the day, there were a female and male spirits in the house. They were holding hands and made their exit through the living room wall.

I often wonder if other indigo children go through the same dilemma that I do. I always wanted to try to at least reach one indigo child. With today's technology, I am sure that I would be able to contact a few like me.

It then crossed my mind that I would probably get all sorts of nonsense thrown at me. I have enough as it is now. I do not want to create more nonsense coming my way. Halloween night is the worse-- prank calls, kids playing tricks; if they only knew there are real ghosts all around them.

Chapter 10

I was having a conversation with a friend about me being an indigo child, and when did I become aware that I could sense someone was going to die.

"Boy, you are testing my brain. To answer that question my friend, I need to access my vault of memories, have a beer… it might take some time. Do you see any smoke coming out of my ears yet?

"Yes."

"I am trying to open the vault but I lost my key. There you go. I remember one night, I was watching television with my dad. Back then I was a young punk; a rebel without a cause."

My friend replied.

"Now you are an old punk."

"Very funny. So anyway, as I was saying before being rudely interrupted by a sarcastic comment, my dad was watching the news, I could feel that the anchorman would die in a very short time. I did not say a word to anyone in fear of being ridiculed."

"Yes. I know it does not take much nowadays to be ridiculed."

"Four days later, I turned on the television to watch the news. I was curious to see if my hunch was right, and there it was… the television station was doing a tribute for their beloved anchorman of thirty years; apparently, he died in his sleep. I do not want to be morbid, but my opinion to pass away in your sleep is the best way to go."

"Really? For real? He died in his sleep?"

"Yes, for real. At the time, I shook it off as a coincidence. Come to think of it, there were a few more incidents which, I would say, it was another coincidence. Remember when I used to be a non-believer in that kind of stuff?"

"Yes. I remember mister hotshot dismissing everything with smartass comments; until one night, someone came knocking at your bedroom door. You ran to mommy."

"Alright. Why don't we take a side road, get off the highway of bad memories and talk about the good times we had growing up. Want another beer?"

When out in public running errands, evening out with friends, or at a sporting event, etc., I can feel that an individual, for example, in the crowd will die in a very short time.

When I am talking to someone on the phone, I can feel he or she will be gone from this world in a short period of time; that is why I often decline an invitation to go out and have fun. I hate the fact when I get the feeling that someone will die.

My biggest problem is dealing with the spirit of a child-- it really bothers me. I have some difficulty to shake it off. One day, I had to deal with a little girl who did not want to go. She wanted to stay with her mom and dad, and play with her super mario games.

A lady once told me she was rushed to the hospital because of a heart attack. The doctors revived her three times.

"I did not feel or see anything but total darkness. I did not understand why, because my mother-in-law died on the operating table. They were able to revive her."

"Okay, and then what?"

"The funny thing is, she saw white doors with gold trimmings. Her mom and several relatives were smiling. Can you tell me why for me it was total darkness and not for my mother-in-law?"

"I am sorry, I cannot tell you why. Maybe, a priest would be able to help you find the reason that it was not the same experience for you and your mother-in-law. I have no clue why it was different for you and your mother-in-law."

"Sorry, my ass. You cannot answer a simple question. You are fake."

As I was walking away, she yelled.

"I will tell everybody not to trust you because you're a con artist."

I turned around, walked to the lady. My face was maybe ten inches from her face.

"I have been more than patient with you. I am only going to tell you once, be careful what you say."

"Why are you threatening me?"

"I am only telling you to be careful what you say."

"That's a threat, you know."

"You can take it which way you want, I do not give a damn. You mentioned the word ass, if I am not mistaken. Well, for what I can see, your ass is large enough to put all of your comments, shove them where the sun doesn't shine."

I could still hear her yelling at me when I got into my car and drove away. Peace and quiet is rare in my neck of the woods, always something that I need to deal with a nitwit like her and bad entities. Some days, I wish I could find an area to hide and not be bothered. If I ever find such a place, I would make it my home and never come back.

They say, be careful what you wish for. I wish ,wish wish, wish, wish, wish, as the situations increase, finding a place to hide, it's like finding a needle in a haystack. On occasions, when I meet people, they ask questions just to be nasty, or condescending. I can see evil in their eyes. One of those dumb questions that one gentlemen in particular was asking,

"Do you own a black cat? Does that mean, you're a warlock? You know, cats, especially black ones, have something to do with Satan. Did you know that?"

"Are you pulling my leg? I hope that you are not serious?"

I continued on my way. He came up to me and said,

"Do not walk away when I ask you a question."

"I am sorry. I must have misunderstood because all I am hearing are dumb comments, not worth answering."

"Are you calling me dumb?"

"No, I am calling you a dumbass. You should listen to yourself babbling. If you always babble nonsense like you are doing now, no one will listen to you and do the same as I am doing right now, walking away."

He looked at me for a few seconds and walked away.

I watched him walk away. What a waste of a good soul; what a nincompoop. This kind of confrontation, the paranormal activities have affected my wife's health.

"I know the psychic told you that my health would improve which it did get better, but dealing with the stress, worrying, lack of sleep, they are starting to affect my health."

"I know. Some days I can see signs of distress in your face. I am really trying hard to not let things bother you but it's not easy."

"I can't help but worry, but I am not going anywhere."

I was waiting to see my family doctor for my yearly checkup. While I was seated in the waiting room, his secretary which I have known for years, waved at me to join her in the hallway.

"If you don't mind, I need to talk to you in private."

"Lead the way, my dear."

"Thank you. Follow me."

We went into her office, closed the door.

"Grab a chair. Don't worry, you will not miss your appointment. I want to talk to you about my daughters. As you well know, they are both pregnant."

"Yes. I am aware that both your girls are pregnant."

"My oldest is having a very complicated pregnancy, her due date is in a month. I am very worried for both my daughters and the babies."

"Can I put my hand on your shoulder?"

"Yes, of course. Please do."

It took a few minutes for me to be able to have a clear vision because I had to get through her in order to connect with her daughter.

"What I was be able to see, remember, things can change. I have no control over the changes that might occur."

"Yes, I know."

"Your daughter will give birth to a healthy, bouncing baby but not without problems; but she will prevail. The new mom and baby will go home and be as snug as a bug in a rug."

"Thank you. My youngest daughter is only in her second month into her pregnancy; so far so good, no complications as of yet. I hope everything will go well for her."

"I need to again put my hand again on your shoulder."

"Go ahead."

Again, it took me a few minutes.

"No need to worry, your daughter will give birth to a healthy baby. Yes, there will be bumps on the road but she will cross the bridge when she gets there."

When the baby of her oldest daughter was born, she called me to say thank you. She called again after the birth of her second grandchild.

"I am so happy, thank you. I now have two beautiful granddaughters."

"You are welcome, but you should be thanking god and the medical staff at the hospital."

"It's already done. I want to thank you again for reassuring all of us. It gave us that extra push that we needed; my husband is so ecstatic , I don't think that he has come back down to earth yet."

"If he does not come back to earth, he will be at the elms of a spaceship instead of his truck. It makes me happy knowing that I was able to help."

My happy moment was short lived. After the phone call, I made my way to the kitchen to get a glass of water to quench my thirst. I was punched in the stomach.

"Show yourself… or are you too much of a coward to do so?"

He did show himself. Standing no more than five feet from me was a full body entity, the shape of a human-- dark brown colored short legs, long arms, big hands, a small mouth and nose. There was some kind of liquid dripping from his nose and into his mouth.

He looked at me with his big yellow eyes. I am sure that he was able to see right through me-- small ears, no horns. There was something crawling on his head. He looked at me straight in the eyes for maybe twenty seconds, and shoved me with my back hitting the back of a solid oak chair. He started growling and laughing. I have never heard a laugh that loud before. He then vanished.

He left behind an awful stench. I have to admit I was shaking in my boots. I was not scared, but worried on what he might do next. A few minutes later, my wife came home from work. First thing she said,

"My goodness! What is going on? You're as white as the snow outside. For the first time, I see a worried look in your eyes. Are you going to be alright? What is that awful smell? Do you want me to bring you to the clinic?"

I declined.

"No doctor will be able to remedy the situation that I experienced a few minutes ago."

I proceeded on filling her in with the details. I have to be honest, it took me a couple of days to get back on track.

I am plagued with bad luck as per Father Joseph. It's because of all the negativity around me brought by the entities that keep harassing me. My guardian angel can only do so much. An angel came to me and whispered in my ear.

"Do not give up. we are side by side on the battlefield along with your guardian angel. We try very hard to keep you safe. We will not let anything bad happen to you."

"What about my bad luck and injuries?"

"Yes, you do get some bad luck, or suffer injuries. We cannot always win. We are battling powerful dark forces. As long as you keep helping spirits go to heaven and do good deeds, they will not stop trying to inflict pain and injuries."

I guess the dark force will be a thorn in my side for quite some time to come. I am not ready to throw in the towel for many moons to come. I am too young to retire.

My mom's sister, my dear aunt was diagnosed with a terminal cancer. She was terrified at the prospect of dying. In her final days, I went to her house to reassure her that I will guide her until she is in heaven. She wanted to be at home for her final days and her family by her bedside.

"You sure you won't forget?"

"No worries, I will be here."

"I am counting on you."

"Yes and I know for a fact that uncle, the love of your life, it is cancer that took him away from you. He will be waiting for you."

The day she passed away, I was at her bedside holding her hand. Her final words to me where,

"Do not let go of my hand."

In her final hours, my aunt's family were by her bedside weeping.

"Be happy for me. I will be pain free and with your dad. I will be waiting for all of you, someday we will all be together in paradise."

She turned and looked at me. I put her tiny hand in mine.

"I have both hands holding on to you."

She closed her eyes, fifteen minutes after closing her eyes. She said in a very weak voice.

"Here he comes."

A few minutes later, she was gone.

"Your dad was waiting for your mom when she entered in heaven."

One of my cousins said,

"I heard my mom say, 'here he comes'."

"Yes. She could see your dad coming towards her."

"Thank you for guiding our mom to heaven. She knew she would be safe with you by her side."

"No need to thank me, we are family. I was happy to be by her side."

"We will see you at the funeral."

"Absolutely."

A lady friend was having problems with dark shadows in her home. I advised her to burn a white candle. I gave her a wooden cross that was blessed and dipped in holy water.

"Hang the cross in an area or room where the dark shadows are manifesting."

She followed my advice; did what I told her to do. A few days later, she told me that the activity had stopped.

I met with a former co-worker. He wanted to talk about his wife that was gravely ill. He wanted to know if I could see his wife recuperating, be well again, or if the end was near. I did what I usually do-- put my hand on his shoulder.

"I am so sorry, my friend, to tell you to spend as much time as possible with your wife. The end is near. I feel for you. I wish I could tell you otherwise. I cannot tell you what day or week, but it is soon. I really feel for you."

"The doctors told me the same thing. By talking to you, I was hoping that you would see a better outcome."

"I am grieving for you."

"I know you are. We worked together for ten years, long enough to get to know you. I know that you are sincere, thank you for being honest with me."

"I cannot tell you that she will overcome the disease and make a full recovery. You put your trust in me. My conscience will never allow me to do such a thing, or give you false hope."

"That would be a cruel and devastating thing to do."

We shook hands.

"My thoughts and prayers are with you."

His wife died six weeks later.

Again, I went to see Father Joseph because one spirit indicated to me that he did not need any help because he has taken the route before to get to heaven. Father Joseph explained.

"Some souls plan for reincarnation to come back amongst the living; and sometimes they come back as animals. That is why animals have souls."

"Now, I understand why my newborn baby crawled in his bassinet. I could see my grandfather's face instead of my son's face. My grandfather looked at me, and he was gone; and I was able to see my baby's face again.

"He wanted to show me he was keeping his word. One night, not long after his funeral, he visited me and said, 'he would be back'."

"He came back to let you know that he was okay and used your son as a gateway."

"I understand. One more thing, I get a lot of déjà vu… you know places, flashbacks."

"Yes, you have an old soul. Do you recall the time you were hypnotized?"

"Yes."

"Well, déjà vu… have you ever recognized a place as if you have been there before but it's the first time that you visit the place? They are memories from previous lives, some are awakened by hypnosis."

"I had some deja vu before being hypnotized."

"Yes, you did. What I meant was, some places can only be remembered with hypnosis. Do the spirits continue to use the light to communicate with you?"

"Yes."

"When they communicate, they are sending you a message that a spirit is on his way or be careful with the black entities."

"Yes. When I receive a warning, I go in overdrive to be ready for whatever is on the way."

My bad luck has not taken a break. The foundation of my house cracked in three different places; human waste backed up in the basement three weekends in a row. While driving home in a bad snow storm, a chunk of ice fell from an overpass, hit my windshield which resulted in a broken wiper on the driver's side.

I stopped on the side of the road to put a rag to help keep my windshield clean so I could navigate my way home. It was awkward. I had to stop; I do not know how many times to clear the snow that accumulated on the windshield. Visibility was next to zero. Boy was I a happy camper when I made it home safe and sound.

One day while driving home, when I rounded a corner, I came upon a pickup truck with its box full of old boards with nails. The driver neglected to cover its load. One board flew off the load and landed right in front of my car. I had no time to avoid the board, which resulted in a flat tire. The tire was done to many punctures to repair.

I could write more situations. I could write a book referring only on the bad luck that comes my way. Father Joseph said, he understood… but not much can be done to prevent bad luck from happening. He advised me to be brave and wished me good luck .

One evening when I arrived home, my wife told me while watching television. She started hearing weird voices coming from the television. She pressed the power off option on the remote, waited a few minutes and pressed the on button. Everything was back to normal. From the corner of her eye, she spotted black shadows walking in the hallway.

While she was filling me in on the details, we both stopped talking. We could hear loud growls coming from the bathroom. I said to my wife,

"Maybe one of the black shadows is constipated."

I took a peek in the bathroom. To no avail, they were gone. Later in the evening, we were watching a movie and we could hear yelling in the basement. I got my ever-expanding butt, off the couch to investigate again. I came up empty.

One night, I was sitting in the living room by myself-- no television. Trying to make sense of a lot of things going on in my life. I felt a little depressed. I could smell a whiff of my dad's aftershave. I let him know that I was going to be alright. I was doing a bit of soul searching, I needed to recharge my batteries.

"Thank you, Dad. It warms my heart knowing that you and mom are keeping an eye on me."

My parents needed to keep an eye on me while growing up; I was no angel-- I caused them a lot of grief. We were seldom on the same page. Here, they are still looking out for me from heaven. When you have kids, it's a job for life and the afterlife. I want to make them proud. It gives me a reason to stay the course, continue to accomplish the tasks I was sent to do.

One night before going to snooze land, I put a tape recorder in the living room and one in the basement, both capable of recording for ninety minutes. It captured unbelievable different tones of voices, weird noises, evil voices, some growling.

Some nights, I sit alone in the dark with only the bathroom light on; giving me enough light to see for me to maneuver and save me from banging my toes on furniture. I hear a lot of white noise, and weird noises. I see things that makes me scratch my head in disbelief.

Some nights before going to bed, I spread some white powder on the floor. It never fails in the morning there are always different sets of footprints especially around our bed. One night, I tried something different. I spread some white powder throughout the house, rubbed holy water all over the bedroom door frame and some salt on the floor.

In the morning, I saw different sets of footprints where I spread the powder on the floor but none in the bedroom. The footprints ended at our bedroom door. At night before going to bed, I rub the bedroom door frame with holy water and salt on the floor-- it is now a ritual for me. I know as long as I keep helping spirits, I will always have company.

Chapter 11

My best friend's mother was very sick. My friend dropped me a line to let me know that his mother passed away. I was not surprised and surprised at the same time. I was unable to understand why she did not come to me for guidance.

There must be a good reason. She would always pick my brain, to make sure to guide her in the right direction. I would say"No worries, I will make sure you go directly to heaven".

I drove to my friend's house to see how he was holding up. As soon as I entered his house, I was overcome by a strange, bizarre sensation that I could not put my finger on what it meant. It was eating me inside not knowing. My friend said a few times.

"Are you okay? You look as if you are lost."

"I am fine. My emotions are starting to kick in."

The following day, it hit with me like a ton of bricks. His dad's journey on this earth will end in the coming days. The night before his mother's funeral, his dad was sleeping at my friend's place. Around four o' clock in the morning, his dad woke up my friend to let him know he was suffering from chest pains and a hard time catching his breath.

He was rushed to the hospital , he passed away early in the morning. The funeral for his mother was postponed. Arrangements were made for a double funeral. The priest let my friend know that his mom came to get his dad so they could go to heaven holding hands.

Married fifty two years, one could not live without the other. She could not wait for her husband to join her in heaven.

I now understand why his mom did not come to me for guidance. She did not want to cross over without her hubby of fifty two years. I was able to guide them both together in heaven.

Every year, a Sunday mass is held at the local cemetery to honor the loved ones that passed away in the past year. When the mass is over, a family member who lost a loved one releases a white balloon to signify that their loved one's spirit is in heaven.

My friend who lost both parents released two white balloons. Those who attended the mass were amazed, both balloons remained side by side until they disappeared into the clouds. His mom and dad wanted to show him that they were together in heaven.

If you walk by a cemetery or visiting the grave of a loved one, when everything is quiet, take the time to listen. Like I said before, you can hear whispering. The spirit of a little girl made its way to me for guidance. She passed away a little while back; an evil entity would not let her go to heaven.

I called Father Joseph. Her soul followed me to see the priest. He performed a special ceremony using candles, a cross and holy water.

The ceremony was new to me. He prayed out loud while lighting five candles. He was on his knees with both arms in the air. He tossed some holy water all around him. Silence for a couple of minutes, he stood up and raised the cross towards the sky.

The ceremony lasted about five minutes. He was able to release the stranglehold the entity had on the little girl, unabling her to go see god. The spirit of the little girl was able to enter in heaven.

I was in the process of asking Father Joseph a question when the black entity in question attacked Father Joseph. The entity pushed him to the ground and was shaking him like a leaf on a branch that is being violently shaken by the wind. His glasses went flying.

I was able to get close enough to throw holy water in the direction of the attack. I recited a prayer out loud. Father Joseph was finally able to shove his crucifix in the face of the entity. The entity finally released his grip, looked at me, pushed me to the ground, then vanished.

I inquired if Father Joseph needed medical help.

"I am okay. A few scratches, a headache from the shaking. A few aspirins will take care of my headache. "

"Do you want me to escort you to the door?"

"No thank you, I am fine. Thank you for helping me."

"Anytime, Father. Was this the first time for this kind of attack or it is common? It is a first for me."

"No. It is not common for that kind of attack. These events are more relevant to hauntings."

"For me it is the first time that a spirit has come to me in such a way."

"Be on the lookout. There might be more that will come your way."

"Next time, I will know what to do."

When Father Joseph said his goodbye, I noticed two white shadows near me.

"Do not be surprised if you see them again. They come to lend a hand."

"Did you know they were here?"

"Yes, I did."

I turned around; both shadows were gone. Later that evening, the black shadow that was preventing the little girl's spirit to go to the light and cross over, made sure that I would remember how aggressive he can be when manifesting.

I was relaxing; listening to music. He came out of nowhere. He hit me in the back of the head and scratched my neck. I turned around to face him. I made a gesture to make sure he could see the cross that

I never remove from my neck, solely for this purpose-- to protect me when entities get aggressive with me. He laughed when he saw the cross.

I hurried to my bedroom to get a candle and some sage. He beat me to it. When I entered the room, I could smell rotten flesh. He was standing at the foot of the bed, growling. He was preventing me from reaching the candles and the sage that was on the dresser. My wife's quick thinking saved the day.

She lit a candle in the kitchen and came running with the candle and some sage in her hands. He looked at my wife, pointing his fingers or whatever they are in her direction, and vanished.

"I was not aware there was sage in the kitchen."

"Yes, remember we stored some in the kitchen cabinet?"

"No, sorry. I do not recall that we keep candles and sage in the kitchen."

"It's a good thing we did it; came in handy tonight."

"It sure did. Without your help, I might still be in battle against the entity. What we should do is keep some sage in every room in the house for easy access."

We needed to spray some Febreze to get rid of that awful odor. I let the candle burn, took the burning sage to again attempt to cleanse the house one more time. It worked for at least the remainder of the evening, no more disruptions.

Over the years, I noticed that I get a feeling as if an invisible force is pushing me to go for a ride or a walk. It never fails that I arrive upon an emergency situation that people need help. Same scenario if I am delayed or running late to get to my destination.

I also noticed that I am less patient with certain individuals when responding to an emergency or even people asking me questions. I have more and more trouble to tolerate pesky people that keep nagging me for whatever reasons. The public is now more reluctant to approach me.

They warn people to be careful what they say to me, *he has a short fuse, it does not take much for him to be annoyed.* My friends now call me the spark plug. I am getting at the point of being mentally and physically exhausted. I am trying very hard to adapt but sometimes life throws you a curve ball.

I went on a fishing trip with friends. On our way home, we decided to stop at a popular water hole for a drink. While enjoying a cold refreshing beer, I noticed a man that never took his eyes off me. I told my friends.

"Here we go again for crying out loud. The man sitting a few tables from us keeps looking at me. Shit man here he comes."

Facing me he had this to say.

"You know something about me that I do not know myself. I can sense it, you better tell me."

I replied.

"First of all like, I say to everyone to stop trying to intimidate me. It does not work, it only fires me up when people such as yourself, think that by having an attitude, will get what you want."

He was standing in front of me with his mouth wide open.

"It blows my mind when I think people can get what they want by using intimidation. Now, please change your attitude and lower your voice. Is it liquid courage that makes you talk this way or is it the real you talking?"

By then, every patron in the bar were listening.

"Do you always introduce yourself the same way that you introduced yourself to me?"

"Yes and no. Only sometimes when I am in a bad mood, I drink and I get aggressive."

"I hope for your sake that you are not always in a bad mood when you drink ."

"I have to admit, my attitude got me in trouble more than once. My wife keeps asking me when will I ever learn?"

"Do you still want to know what you think I know? I have never seen you before in my life. You might not like what I have to say, what makes you think that it`s something concerning you?"

"First of all, my name is…"

I interrupted him,

"I do not want to know your name, we can remain anonymous."

"Okay, have it your way and yes I do know for some reason. I just know that you know something concerning me. As soon as you walked in, an uneasy feeling came over me that you know something about me."

His wife walked over to join us.

"What is going on?"

He looked at his wife.

"This man has a revelation concerning me."

She looked totally confused and said,

"Ok."

"What I am about to divulge here today, please do not hold it against me. I am only a messenger."

"I understand. No worries."

"Are you sure?"

"Yes, I am sure. Now, can you tell me what it is you need to tell me? It's driving me crazy not knowing."

By then, everyone in the bar was listening.

"Can we talk outside?"

Some bar patrons followed us outside. I told them to keep their distance.

"What I have to say does not concern any of you. Alright, here it goes. Remember you wanted to know. In a very short period of time, two of your family members will die. I cannot tell you who or when."

They both looked at me in disbelief.

"You insisted on knowing."

"You are full of shit."

They jumped in their truck and drove away. When I went back in the bar, my friends were waiting for me.

"No rest for the wicked, it follows you everywhere."

"Yes, I know. You guys are right, no rest for the wicked. There is no other way to put it."

Everyone was making their way in my direction.

"No need for any of you to come to my table for information because it is none of your business. Please give me some breathing room so that I can finish enjoying my beer."

Some were upset with me.

"How would you like it if any of you guys speak to me, and moments later, I spill the beans to everyone? How would you like that?"

Some responded,

"We would not like it at all."

"Same for him, what's good for the goose is good for the gander."

As luck would have it, the following weekend, the man and his son were involved in an ATV accident-- they both died. His wife gave a statement to the police that I jinxed her husband and her son, by putting a curse on her family. The police came to my house.

"I did not have anything to do with the accident. If you are looking for a culprit who is responsible for the accident, you are barking up the wrong tree."

"Relax, sir. We are here to hear your side of the story."

"Relax, it's easy for you to say. I certainly did not jinx or put a curse on anybody, that`s ridiculous . First of all, I do not know these people."

"You had a conversation with them a week ago."

"He was the one that approached me last weekend in a bar. He told me that I knew something about him and insisted, so I told him. When I did tell him, he said that I was full of shit and took off in his truck. I truly am sorry for her loss."

One of the cops said,

"Do you know that it's illegal to practice voodoo magic? "

"I hope you guys are not implying that I practice black magic."

"Did it bother you when he said you were full of shit?"

"Not one bit, believe me. I have been called worse. *Full of shit* is mild compared to what the public has been dishing out over the years. I tell people what they want to know; if they cannot accept the truth, it's their problem, not mine."

"We cannot find any proof that you were involved in the accident."

"Of course not. Like I said, I only saw them once: it was last weekend. I did not know who they were, or where they came from. Some blabbermouth, squealed on me and gave her my name"

"How do you know, someone gave her your name?"

"Although I should be aware by now that people will talk no matter the consequences spreading gossip, if everyone would mind their own business, there would be a lot less turmoil in the world that we live in."

"She is convinced that you had something to do with the accident. Okay we are done here. Sorry for the inconvenience, but we need to investigate every lead in a case."

"Yes I know."

"I do not know how she is going to absorb the fact that you had nothing to do with the accident. So you are on of those fortune tellers?"

"That's what they say."

We shook hands and they were on their way.

"Boy, will it ever end? "

I am swamped with. people who want to know why some spirits reincarnate and some do not. I keep repeating the same answer. *I do not know, go talk to a priest he might be able to answer the question.* One particular individual replied,

"You deal almost everyday with that kind of stuff and you do not know the answer, or is it because you do not want to tell me?"

"Why would I do that? I simply do not know. Like I said, go see a priest or purchase a book on reincarnation. With a book, the answer might be under your nose and not know it."

"Why are you saying that it might be under my nose and not see it?"

"No offense, but look at the size of your nose-- it covers two-thirds of your face. Now, you know go home and leave me alone."

"No need to insult me."

"Bye bye, and good luck on your quest to find an answer to your question."

I came home a bit flustered,

When I walked in the house, my wife saw my flustered face.

"What's wrong?"

"Nothing."

"Ok, now I understand you had to deal with one of them today."

"Yes, one of them."

"So anyway, earlier in the day, there was a smell in the kitchen as if someone lit a match."

"I will be darn a ghost that smokes."

The next morning, I spotted two black shadows at the foot of the basement stairs-- they were both looking in my direction. I could hear an evil voice talking to me. I could not understand a word he said. They again looked at me for a few seconds and vanished. There was constant knocking in the house for the remainder of the day.

My wife was rushed to the hospital in critical condition, because of an accident while horseback riding. While she was in the intensive care unit, I prayed asking my mom, dad, and sister for help and to show a sign they were listening.

The room filled with warm air, I could see a silhouette hovering over her bed for a couple of minutes. I could not see who answered my prayers, but I said a *big thank you and to come again.*

I was at her bedside twenty-four hours a day. After a few days, I came home to take a shower, pack a bag, have a good night sleep. The doctor assured me if there were any changes in her condition, they will call me. I called my sister if she could continue to take care of the cats and the dog.

I was trying to relax before going to bed. The phone rang, on my caller id, I could see the hospital phone number. I answered the phone, all I could hear was gibberish. I hung up, called the hospital if someone had tried to reach me. The nurse put me on hold when she came back on the phone.

"I checked with the nurses and doctors. No one tried to call you."

"Ok, thank you for taking the time to check for me."

I was puzzled as to why the phone would ring with gibberish at the other end of the call. A little later in the evening, the phone rang again, and again, and again. I did not want to take the phone off the hook in case the hospital would call.

Every call, the hospital number would appear on the caller id. I was dumbfounded at how the entities knew the hospital might call me. The only way possible if one of the entities has the task to follow me everywhere I go. Everytime I answered the phone, I heard weird noises. They were playing with me.

After several more calls, I stopped answering the phone and let the calls go to my voicemail. Finally the calls stopped. When I listened to the messages, I could hear voices-- some growling that gave me the creeps. I deleted the messages and went to bed. I was exhausted when my head hit the pillow. I was already snoring.

I was awakened by a very loud male voice coming from the hallway. I jumped out of bed to go take a look, as usual-- nothing. I crawled back into bed. When I was about to fall back asleep, I was slapped on the head. I lit a candle and prayed. I let the candle burn. When the candle was done, I was finally able to go to sleep.

The next morning, I noticed fresh scratches on both arms. The light was flashing on my answering machine. I picked up the phone in a hurry, maybe the hospital called and I did not hear the phone ring. To my surprise, it was the same messages that I deleted.

The entities have found a way to not be seen or heard by my dog. After spending eighteen days in the hospital, my wife was feeling well enough to come home. She was resting on the couch watching television; she was kissed on the cheek. She looked at me.

"It's my grandfather. A few minutes before being kissed on the cheek, I saw my grandfather through you.

"Funny, I did not feel a thing. Are you sure? Because I did not leave the chair."

"Yes, I am one hundred percent sure. I know you did not leave the chair, he used you as a gateway to get to me."

"Ok, if you say so."

Later in the evening, I saw a bright light the size of a ping pong ball. My wife indicated to me that it was her grandmother checking if everything was okay with her.

For about two weeks, my wife would see a white shadow looking down on her and exit through the kitchen door. My wife knew it was her grandmother that was keeping an eye on her to make sure everything was going well with her recovery. The last time my wife saw the white shadow hovering above her, my wife was relaxed. The room was peaceful, she fell asleep.

One evening while watching television, I was dozing off in my chair. I was shoved by a black shadow. After waiting a little while for his next move, I fell asleep. When I woke up, I was covered with bugs. I ran into the kitchen to get a can of bug spray.

Thank god, I was able to kill them all. In the meantime, my wife who was sleeping on the couch woke up, wanting to know what was going on. She freaked out when she saw all the dead bugs on the floor. I can never get a moment of peace and quiet.

Chapter 12

Indigo children always dream when asleep, no different for me. If I wake up two, or three times at night, it is always a different dream when I fall asleep again.

Often in my dreams, I am lost at work or if I go for a break, I cannot find my way back to my desk. When I am done working, I cannot find my car. I have to hitchhike in order for me to go home.

Another dream, my marriage is falling apart or I am delayed getting home. I have no way to reach my wife to let her know that I am on my way home. Another bizarre dream-- I can fly.

At a factory, I am stuck between industrial machinery; I argue with strangers, friends, family most of the time with my mom. Last but not the least, I wear a medical device on my face.

(Flying unaided: dreams of flying through the air convey a sensation of ease and elation; fully detached from preoccupations of the material world. Dreamers may feel on an exalted spiritual plane, at one with the universe. Some people reporting such dreams claim to have felt a sense of being in touch with their own immortality. Flying may also point to a need to get emotional bearings by taking an overview of the many aspects on your life.)

(Fighting and arguing: a dreamer lashing out indiscriminately to others around them may be struggling to fight undersirable impulses to their conscious or unconscious minds. Violence against an older person can suggest resistance to a figure of authority; for me it would be the devil.)

(Lost: this may be accompanied by unanticipated feelings or resentment toward our loved ones. It is not uncommon for bereaved people to feel. In

addition to the sorrow of their loss, a painful sense that the deceased has chosen to abandon them. You can find all the information in the book of **1,001 Dreams and their Meaning**.)

For me that's why in my dreams, I am always stuck between machinery, unable to move, or always arguing with someone--it can be a stranger or a family member. It is like a tug of war between two worlds. Entities can use dreams to manifest.

That is why I feel stuck somewhere or flying with angels. I travel through one galaxy to another, between the world of the deceased and the living. As per Father Joseph, it is not a dream I really travel through galaxies. It pretty well explains my dreams and reality.

One of my friends called; he needed a hand, programming his new cell phone. When I entered my friend's house, I sensed something was not right.

"A few days ago, my wife was diagnosed with colon cancer."

I put my hand on her shoulder and closed my eyes. After a couple of minutes, I opened my eyes and removed my hand.

"You have a very bumpy road ahead of you, but you will make it. You will win the fight against that dreaded disease."

She did go through a rough ride and made it to the finish line--she is now cancer free. The only inconvinience she now has is a bag attached on her side. She is okay with that, she said,

"It is better to be alive this way than not being alive."

One of my close friends moved away for a job. I ran into his brother, he inquired if I was aware that his brother, my friend, suffered a serious heart attack.

"No, I did not know."

"He is scheduled tomorrow morning for a complicated heart surgery. In a few hours I will be on the way to the hospital . A five hour drive."

Like always, I did my ritual .

"Tell him not to worry, he is going to make it. He will be back on his feet in no time. I am sending all my positive vibes his way."

"Funny that I ran into you. Before leaving, I was going to call you. I will tell him what you said, I am sure it will give him more confidence heading into surgery. I will keep posted."

"Please, and safe travels my friend."

He gave me a thumb's up and was on his way. Like I said before, I am often at the right place at the right time. My friend made a full recovery and back at work. Father Joseph once told me, chance meetings or emergencies why you are always johnny on the spot-- their guardian angel communicates with my guardian angel.

"That is why you are often drawn to be or go somewhere with people in distress. Like the time you told me you were coming out of a store, the parking lot was icy. The lady in front of you slipped on the ice and broke her hip and leg."

"Yes, poor lady was yelling she could not take the pain."

"The young lady involved in a car accident; remember that day. You decided to go visit your parents you came upon the accident. The senior citizen caught in the revolving doors at a department store. Do I need to say more?"

Black shadows, entities are still having fun at my place-- doors opening, closing by themselves, constant smell. I once told the entities, they could use the shower to scrub themselves clean.

It would eliminate the stink they leave behind when they exit the premises. Fluctuating temperatures, loud bangs in the kitchen in the basement anywhere in the house for that matter.

Black shadows always taunting me, randomly inflicting pain. Shadow devils on the ceiling watching my every move. I asked my mom, dad and sister for help to deal with a very difficult situation.

"You guys should have a bird's eye view from up there."

For some reason that day, my request for help fell on deaf ears. I was dealing with bad, angry spirits. They were relentless, I had to do battle on my own which is not easy. They gave me a good run for my money. One evening, I am convinced they pulled numbers out of a jar for each one to have their turn to drive me crazy. Good timing for a visit from Father Joseph, he told me,

"They were bad angry people when alive-- they bring their attitudes, bitterness with them in the afterlife."

I wanted my parents and sister to show me a sign they were listening to my request for help. The lights blinked twice. With their help along with Father Joseph's help, I was able to make some headway with the grumpy spirits. Father Joseph was about to leave when I popped him the question, why a few days ago my request for help was not answered.

"Wow, what a question. To be honest my friend, I have no clue why your request for help was not answered."

"Oh, well… one more for the books, another mystery with no answers. So anyway, thanks again Father for your help."

A few days later, my wife was visiting relatives. When I came home from work, the first thing I noticed, photos of my parents and my deceased sister where on the floor; picture frames smashed to pieces.

Someone or something was not happy with my associates to put an end to their manifesting. A few days later, my wife came home from visiting her relatives.

"Did I miss something while I was gone?"

"No. Same old, same old."

I received a call from my neighbor, her husband was in a medical crisis. I told my wife to call 911. I rushed across the street to help my neighbor until the ambulance arrived. My wife was standing outside in our driveway, when she noticed a grey shadow with a black cape and hoodie at the end of our driveway.

"What do you want?"

He responded to her question by pointing in my neighbor's direction.

"You are wasting your time. My neighbor is not going anywhere except to the hospital."

The grey shadow ignored my wife. After five minutes, he vanished. With the grey shadow gone, my neighbor was feeling a lot better. The ambulance arrived, my neighbor's wife told the paramedics that her husband was now feeling a lot better and there was no need to see a doctor.

The paramedics persuaded my neighbor to go to the hospital as a precaution. My wife was still outside waiting for me to come home. She told me about the grey shadow.

"I told him, he was wasting his time and he eventually vanished."

I now have a pretty good idea but not a hundred percent convinced why my neighbor was feeling a lot better when the paramedics arrived. This event still baffles me as to why the grey shadow was standing outside, pointing in the direction of my neighbor's house. If he wanted his soul, he did not put up a good fight.

I beg the question, was he responsible for my neighbor's medical condition? What was his purpose for watching? Where did he come from? The entity has not come back since that night.

One night, I was driving on a remote country road. Three entities were in the middle of the road, floating about two feet from the road. They had their back to me. They were not moving. When I was close enough, I was able to see all three were wearing black capes and hoodies.

All three were holding hands. I slowed down almost to a crawl. When I was too close for their liking, they vanished only to reappear about a hundred feet in front of the truck. They were still close enough from each other to hold hands, this time they were facing me. I was not able to get a glimpse of their faces. Again, as I got closer, they vanished.

I went up a hill, I could see a blinking light between the trees. To me, it looked like a street light. I got out of the truck to have a better look. I was able to see a house about fifty feet from the road. The house was dark, nobody was home. By then, I could no longer see the light.

I got back in my truck. As I was driving away, I looked in the rearview mirror-- the light was on again. I was rounding a corner when I saw a moving black shadow with red eyes positioning itself in front of the truck. I drove right through him. I could hear a woman's voice, but I was unable to quite make out what she was trying to tell me. I stopped the truck, turned off the engine-- dead silence.

"Who is it? Do you need anything? Please talk to me, can you please repeat to me what you just said? I was unable to hear you. Why did you come to me at the same time when the black shadow was manifesting in front of the truck?"

Again, nothing but silence. I could not understand what was going on. By then, the shadow was gone. I waited a few more minutes, nothing but silence. I started the truck on my way to my destination.

On my way home, I ventured on the same road hoping to get a repeat performance from earlier in the evening. I could not comprehend what I witnessed. I drove through that stretch of the road still trying to make sense of the events. Nothing but a dark road in front of me. I was baffled.

Is it a phenomenon that I should know or not know about? A message or warning of some kind? It's eating me up inside not knowing. Maybe it's a good thing, I could shed a few pounds. The following night at home we were watching a movie, with scenes people wearing hoodies. I said to my wife,

"There is something bizarre going on with hoodies. The grey shadow with the hoodie in our yard when I was across the street helping our neighbor. Last night, entities with hoodies in the middle of the road, and now, in the movie that we are watching."

When the movie was over, it was still early so we decided to watch another movie. The second movie we were watching, again, people with hoodies. I looked at my wife.

"Am I seeing things or what? A coincidence… I think not. Enough with the hoodies for crying out loud."

Again, I went knocking on Father Joseph's door.

"What is the topic of discussion today?"

"Today, I have another interesting subject to talk about."

I provided him the information about the beings wearing hoodies.

"Interesting. I am sorry to say my dear friend, I am as confused as you are."

Even with further discussion and research in books, we were not able to find a reason for the hoodies. I still do not know what was the purpose of the entities on the road with hoodies; and the two movies with characters in the movies with hoodies. Still a mystery to me.

Later in the day, I was watching television, I got a whiff of something burning on the kitchen stove. As usual nothing, maybe an entity was trying to cook my dinner. Later in the evening, I took my dog outside to do his business. My neighbor's porch light came on, my neighbor's son was walking home in front of my house. The light on his cellphone kept blinking. He looked at me.

"That is weird, that's the first time that my phone has done that."

The light on his phone stopped blinking when he was in the driveway of his house. When I came back in the house, my wife said,

"Come and see this."

There was a white light about the size of a baseball glowing in the corner of our living room a couple of inches from the ceiling. It glowed for a moment and it was gone.

"Boy that was strange. I don't know the meaning of the light."

A few minutes later, my neighbor's porch light came on and off again. I walked over to my neighbor and inquired if there was a timer for his porch light to come on or off. The answer was negative on the timer. He was curious to know why I was asking that question.

"I could have sworn I saw the light blink. Anyway, I am thinking of getting one and I want to know if they are practical and reliable."

"Yes, they are. They are worth the money. There is also an option to turn the lights on or off or use the timer. I did not turn the lights on or off, why did they blink?"

"Probably, bugs in front of the motion sensors."

"No there is no sensor."

"Oh! Well, false alarm. Sorry."

"No worries, goodnight."

I went back home. I said to my wife.

"You know, I think I built this house in the twilight zone."

I went to visit my trusted friend, Father Joseph, for another chat. This time it was concerning the lights.

"I have been doing some thinking about the entities with the famous hoodies that we talked about the other day. Believe me, you keep my brain in overdrive. The one thing that I can think of is that, the entities were preparing to take your neighbor's soul."

"What's that? I don't understand."

"That night, you interfered again in their plan. Maybe, that's why the entities with hoodies came to you with a warning. For me, it is the only logical explanation that I can think of."

"There would be a lesser confusion if they would drop an envelope in the mail; maybe, they cannot afford the price of a stamp. Father, the thing you said about taking my neighbor's soul… none of my neighbors are sick."

"What I meant is the night you ran across the street to help your neighbor."

"Oh yes, maybe… I don't know. It's like the saying, "I see" says, the blind man to his deaf friend."

"The answer about your inquiry for the lights. It's quite possible it was a sign from the powers above that they are watching from a distance."

"I have heard that one before. I which they would be closer, maybe the encounters would be a lot less physical. They would be in my corner a lot sooner."

"I know it can be frustrating but,"

"Sorry for cutting you off but sometimes, I feel like a boxer with no trainer. Nobody in my corner of the ring. As far as I am concerned, I still do not know what to think about the events."

One night, an entity tried to possess me. I was sitting in my recliner in the living room. I got up to go to the kitchen. On my way to the kitchen, everything was turning around me as if I was on a carnival ride. I fell on my ass; my wife came running. After getting up from the floor, I made my way back to my chair.

"Are you alright?"

I remember sitting down in my chair and then I was standing in front of a green steel bridge. I was surrounded by people getting closer and closer. I started to fight them off, I heard my wife calling my name and I was back in my chair. My wife did not know what was happening. She called 911.

"You were fighting something or someone. Your eyes were red and your skin was like pale blue. I yelled at the entity that was trying to possess you. I said, 'you have no right to be here. This is a house of god so, release him.' You did a motion as if someone punched you in the stomach."

"I called out your name at least ten times before you responded and looked at me and when you did, the red eyes and pale blue skin was gone." I was feeling a little dizzy, other than that I was okay. I cancelled the 911 call.

"Wow. Talk about a weird experience."

I was finally able to stand up, walked around the kitchen table a few times, made my way back to the living room. My wife noticed that the chain around my neck with the cross my daughter gave me was missing. She was right, my chain broke during the ordeal. I found the chain on the floor in front of my chair. I picked it up and went into my room to get another chain.

I immediately put another chain around my neck, the cross is one important weapon in my arsenal to do battle against satan and company. My wife was worried about what she witnessed, it really shook her up.

"The ordeal lasted a few minutes. I have never seen anything like it that's why I called 911. I hope I never have to witness that again. You cannot imagine how happy I was when you looked at me and your eyes were back to normal."

Father Joseph got word of my ordeal. He rushed over to my place to make sure a demon did not attach itself to me and take another shot of taking over my body and soul. When he knocked at the door, I was surprised to see it was him.

"Please step in my humble establishment. What brings you here today? Good news, I hope."

"Your bout with the entity the other night."

"Boy… news travel fast in our little town. When we are still on the scene battling a blase, pictures and comments are already on social media."

"First of all, how are you?"

"I am ok, thank you for asking. My wife is worried that there might be a second shot to get me."

"I can very well understand."

"I am one hundred percent certain they tried to fix my wagon by possessing me and have full control over me."

"I do not understand why you did not come and see me."

"To be honest, I really don't know myself; probably too much of a shock for me to be able to talk about the situation I was in. I never expected anything like that. Like the ACDC song says, *it shook me all night long.*"

My wife described to Father Joseph what she saw that evening.

"It scared the living daylight out of me."

"I don't blame you to be scared. From what you told me, it was an attempt of possession. Be on your guard, they may be back for round two."

"I hope not, I do not want to go through that again."

"The circle of people around you, they were there to protect you. They put up a shield between you and the entity. The green bridge was for you to hurry to cross the bridge over a river of holy water. "

"I do not think I even made it to the bridge."

"Your cross was on the floor, the chain broke when you were in the fight of your life. It was not the crowd closing in on you that you were fighting, it was the dark forces. All I can say, be careful! Prepare for the worst and hope for the best."

"Thank you for stopping by. I am a little curious on how you found out about the other night. My plan was to go knocking on your door tomorrow night."

"I had a chat with your sister."

"I will do my best to be ready if there is another attempt like the one a few nights ago, but we all know you cannot be on full alert twenty-four hours a day, seven days a week. That's impossible."

"I know but do your best."

"I always try to do my best."

"I know you do, so long until the next event."

"Yes sir."

When Father Joseph was driving away, we started to hear strange noises. I told my wife.

"Boy it did not take long for them to get out of the gate."

An invisible wolf was howling in the kitchen and puddles of water on the kitchen floor. I did the walkabout throughout the house. I could not find the source where the water came from, every four or five days they come back to entertain us.

Chapter 13

Once in a while, my dear sister that passed away stops by. I get a whiff of her perfume. I wish she could still visit me in the flesh like the good old days.

"I appreciate you checking up on me. I love you my dear sister. I miss you more and more every day, you took the road to heaven way too soon, way too young to leave us. I still have a hard time to accept the fact that you are gone. Not a day goes by that you are not on my mind. Come and visit more often."

I can feel her standing beside me.

"Your visits always bring sad and happy tears: sad that you are no longer with us, and happy that you take the time to let me know that you are always nearby."

We were very close and always there for one another. One night, her daughter was having a gathering of friends; photos where taken. In one of the photos, you can clearly see my sister's silhouette especially her face looking down on her daughter and her friends.

My niece who now owns my parent's house, rents the place to a couple. At night, during the winter months, they hear noise in the basement as if someone is putting firewood in the furnace. They go check and do not see anyone. I let them know,

"That's my dad. One of his workshops was in the basement during the winter months; it was his number one workshop. He always made sure to have enough wood in the furnace to keep his shop and the house warm and cozy."

I was doing volunteer work at an outside event. I was sitting in a tent. It was a nice bright sunny day, perfect weather for outdoor activities. I felt drops of water dripping on my shoulder. I looked up in the sky, I saw two clouds shaped like angels. Participants and people from the crowd stopped what they were in the process of doing, to take photos.

A few days later, I was in my backyard enjoying the sunshine. Over my house, I could see clouds shaped like angels. I call them cloud angels. I guess it was a reminder for me to refresh my memory that angels were never far away.

One evening while having dinner, a female voice whispered in my ear. The whispering turned into howling and then a very loud growl. The notepad on the kitchen counter flew in the air, landed a few feet from me. There was also a smell of burnt toast-- no bread in the toaster. In the bathroom, a full bottle of shampoo split wide open when it hit the floor.

A foul smell in the living room, the sound of someone chocking, the television remote went berserk. I was upset that I could not even enjoy a quiet dinner with my better half without being harassed by a unit of bozos. I was not able to finish my meal. I lost my appetite. I started clearing the table; I dropped a few dishes out of frustration.

I took a deep breath and looked outside the kitchen window; my front porch light blinked a few times, the same for the tail lights on my truck that was parked in the driveway. I looked twice in the direction of the truck to make sure by being upset that my eyes were not playing tricks on me. The truck was locked, the key's in the house.

It was a sign for me not to despair. The angels were there next to me, they were able to chase away the entities. In the past, I would tell my wife some funny quotes about the events, disturbances, not anymore. I told my wife,

"I am like a duck on a pond, everything on the surface looks nice and calm but under the water, the duck's little legs are going a mile a minute. That's the way I feel now. I might look calm but inside, I feel like the ducks little legs helping me to push forward. I feel that way because I am an emotional wreck."

"I wish there was something I could do to help you."

"You are helping me everyday with your support and love. If one day for a reason or another, you say to yourself *'enough is enough I cannot take anymore of this shit'*, please let me know."

"You know when I have something to say, I say it."

"I will find some compromises or stop altogether what I do before you pack your bags and leave me, that would be devastating. That would be like a knockout punch and I am unable to get back on my feet."

"No worries honey, I knew what I was getting into when I met you. One day, if you decide to boot me out of the house by the front door, I will come right back in by the back door. That's how I am devoted to you."

Later in the evening, satan sent a platoon of warriors-- like the Vietnam war. The army would send troops on a search and destroy mission. We had to cope with entities all evening. They say, animals can sense fear, see things that we humans are not able to see or hear. The cats at home often stare in a certain direction. Something caught their attention.

A good majority of the entities do not want to be seen while doing their dirty work, but are unable to hide from the animals.

One evening, the dog were barking. The dog jumped on my lap-- he was shaking. The dog kept on barking. I looked in the direction where the dog was barking. I could not see anything out of the ordinary.

I got up to go to the bathroom, a black entity was standing in the hallway and vanished. I guess one of their favorite games is hide and seek or they are cowards. They are unable to face the music when caught in the act. One night, I was driving home, I noticed a streetlight that was blinking. I slowed down to take a look. I was able to see the face of a close friend.

A fellow firefighter, it was a message from his guardian angel that he needed my help. I rushed to his home. When I entered the house, he looked at me,

"What made you come here? Today is supposed to be your day off."

"Yes, it is my day-off."

As I was making my way to his dad's bedroom,

"Do you have your radio with you?"

"No. When I am off duty, my radio is turned off and I recharge the battery. Your dad needs medical attention."

"Yes, I called 911. The lady who took the 911 call said that our unit was dispatched to help our neighboring fire department. They are on a scene of a very bad multiple vehicular accident; she could not give me an eta."

"No eta."

"They dispatched an ambulance that is thirty minutes away. They are on their way to the hospital with a patient and will be here as soon as they can."

We did what we could with what we had to work with. My friend said,

"I can think of better ways to spend my day-off."

When we entered his dad's bedroom, he was sitting on the side of the bed-- having a hard time breathing and holding his chest. We were able to make him feel more comfortable until the ambulance arrived. After it seemed like an eternity, the ambulance finally arrived. I put my hand on his shoulder.

"Do not worry, you will make a full recovery."

He looked at me.

"Thank you."

"I really appreciate that you came over to give me a hand. Not too bad for a couple of guys on their day off. Thanks again, man."

"Happy to do it. See you in a couple of days at work."

"You betcha buddy."

His dad was rushed to the hospital. He needed a triple bypass heart surgery; two weeks in the hospital and he was back home. He needs to watch what he eats, take his medication, and he will be amongst the living for some time to come.

One evening, I was driving home, I noticed a light coming from the church bell tower; no lights up there. An angel was flying around the tower. A few passersby stopped to look at the flying angel. To me, it was a signal to warn me that I was going to have unwanted nasty visitors.

When the angel vanished, I continued on my way home. I do not call them entities, I call them assholes, ugly, cowards, etc.; a real torn in my side. An entity raised the radio's volume.

The entity tried to take control of the steering wheel. I was able to stop the truck on the side of the road. I quickly rubbed some holy water on the steering wheel, just in case that the malevolent entity would try to take control of the truck one more time. The angel that warned me was right.

Same night while cooking dinner, a loud bang hard enough to partially displace a pot of boiling water off the stove's front burner. I removed the pot from the stove. The pot was given a whack by an unseen coward. I spilled a bit of boiling water on my toes, which resulted with me doing a little dance of pain.

I hope the entity enjoyed the show. I could hear him snickering probably getting high because of my pain. After taking care of my boiling toes, I resumed cooking dinner. While having dinner in the dining room, we could hear some paper shuffling in the kitchen and also as if someone was trying to take a deep breath. I said to my wife,

"We have a jealous ghost."

"What do you mean? "

"It's all falling into place: the shove with the pot of boiling water, now paper shuffling and a deep breath. Our unwelcomed visitor was maybe a chef in the real world of the living."

"Really a chef."

"He is frustrated that I was able to cook a very nice dinner and he is still shuffling the pages of a cookbook."

I yelled out at him.

"You dimwit you remind me of someone who is always the bridesmaid and never the bride."

Later in the evening while watching television, another loud noise in the kitchen. Again, I yelled out,

"It's time for you to go home. It's probably passed your bedtime. Mommy and Daddy will be upset if you're late getting home. Now, be a nice little boy or girl and go home."

Again, my wife said,

"I keep on telling you, you have to stop throwing insults at them-- they might retaliate."

"I do not give a rat's ass if they do."

"A little while back, you were too tired and depressed to call them names and reply with insults."

Three loud bangs in the hallway.

"I might have hit a nerve with my lovely comments."

Another loud bang this time it was behind my chair.

"I hear you knocking but you cannot come in."

When the movie we were trying to watch between the disturbance of the knocks was finally over, we went to bed. When we entered the bedroom, a loud bang on the bedroom wall. I started singing the song *Knocking on Heaven's Door*. The entity must have gone to the school of hard knocks, he sure loves making noise. I guess he went to bed the same time we did. No more knocking, thank goodness.

Once again, I was donating my time for another fundraiser. I was given a job in the canteen. A lady was walking towards the canteen; I could feel sadness and anguish. When at the cash register to pay for her purchases, she noticed that I was looking at her.

"I am sorry for staring but I can sense sadness."

She was making her way towards me.

"Yes, what is it that you're feeling?"

"You want me to tell you? "

"Yes, please do tell me."

"You recently lost someone very close and dear to you, a female about your age with long black air."

"Yes, my best friend since we were kids. She passed away a month ago because of breast cancer."

"I am so sorry for your loss."

"Are you a psychic?"

"No, I am not a psychic but I am an indigo child. We are a bit different than everybody else.

"As a matter of fact, yes I do know a little about indigo kids."

 We talked for a few minutes.

"It's been a pleasure talking to you. I better go rejoin my family. Thank you, goodbye."

"You are quite welcome."

By making the stupid mistake of identifying myself as an indigo child, I opened a new can of worms. She did not waste any time to mention the reason why she was gone for a short period of time.

She mentioned to her family that she was having a conversation with an indigo child. The flood gates opened, her family and friends rushed over wanting to discuss certain issues they were experiencing. Word got around quickly.

I was swamped with questions. My head was spinning in all directions-- the questions where coming non-stop like they were fired from a machine gun. I could not even come close to answer at least one question. I was bombarded with a ton of inquiries. The curiosity of human beings needing to be in the know is beyond me; that's all I can say.

"Please, everybody, stop talking for a second. How do you expect me to answer one single question at the rate they are coming at me? You guys are choking me. I cannot even take a simple breath by drilling me for information, wanting to know everything that is under the sun."

Someone from the crowd shouted.

"We know you have all the answers."

"I am sorry folks, I did not come here to talk about who or what I am. The only thing that I will do is listen to you if you want something from the canteen, otherwise, you are all wasting your time."

The same individual shouted.

"I know why you do not answer our questions. You do not want to do it for free. What if I throw a twenty dollar bill your way, are you going to answer our questions?"

I shouted to the individual.

"Come closer, I will show you what I will do with your money. Believe me, it won't be pleasant. Sorry to be rude but please, all of you, leave me alone."

The crowd finally dispersed. The lady looked at me.

"I am so sorry. I should have kept my mouth shut."

A small group of people remained at the canteen. They were asking my name, my phone numbe and my address.

"Like I said, you are all wasting your time unless you are willing to donate one hundred dollars right here right now. Here is the donation plate, please feel free to donate. Please do not call or come knocking at my door."

One guy shouted,

"You are such an asshole, very rude. A liar full of shit and there is no such thing as an indigo child."

"Listen buddy, I am not the one who came over to smell everybody's farts. You are the type of person that thinks by eating rye bread you will get drunk. Do you have any brothers or sisters?"

"One brother, why do you need to know that?"

"Your mom did not raise too many stupid kids; there are only two of you."

I love using that line. He turned around and walked away, I could tell he was disgusted with me. I should have known not to say anything. Man what was I thinking? Boy, what a brain fart. They will be able to find my phone number and my address. With the public, the less you say, the better it is for you.

Some individuals called me anyway, everyone that took the time to call were not making any sense. I would terminate the call. I was surprised and very happy, no one came knocking at my door.

My sister owns a store. Once in a while, I help her by working the evening shift. The store is equipped with a sensor: When you walk into the store a bell rings to let you know that a customer has entered the store. On several occasions, the bell rang, no customer in the store. I could hear the sound of someone coughing; again, no customer.

"Whoever is coughing, we sell cough syrup. You should not be out causing mischief. Go home dumbass, your going to spread your germs in the store."

I felt a cold breeze pass by me and it was quiet again. A customer walked in, purchased a few items. While paying for her items,

"A slow night."

"Yes, my last customer before you was about a half hour ago."

"Really,"

"Yes."

"But when I walked in the store, I saw a man in the toy department."

"I must have been busy putting stuff on the shelves I did not hear him come in. I will go check if he needs my help. I will be right back. I do not see anybody. Hello."

No answer.

"Maybe he switched aisles. Hello."

Again no answer.

"I could have sworned, I saw a man when I walked in. He was tall and wearing a long a gray coat. I hope that I am not starting to imagine things."

"Sometimes, when we walk into a building, the lights can make us see things… been there done that."

"I guess you are right. I apologize for the false alarm. Goodnight."

"No worries. Goodnight."

I was very well aware that the customer did see an apparition, thinking it was a customer. I was not about to tell her; she might have seen a ghost. Imagine the rumors, and gossip about the store being haunted.

A few minutes later, another customer walked into the store. I struck up a conversation with her. She was very worried about her mom, who was in the hospital; problems with diabetes which damaged her heart.

"The day after tomorrow, the doctors will do a procedure to install a pacemaker."

I inquired if she was on dialysis.

"Not yet. I keep hoping that it does not come to that."

"No need to worry, the procedure will go smoothly with no complications."

"What makes you say everything will go... like you said, smoothly?"

"I just know."

"But why do you know? You don't know her."

"It's a hunch. When it comes to my hunches, I am rarely wrong."

"I hope you are right. My goodness! Look at the time, I need to get going. Thank you, nice talking to you."

"Same here."

After closing the store, I was on my way home. The green traffic light blinked several times. Once home, I warned my wife that a tragedy will occur, within a few days. I do not know where or when, but something will happen. Several days later, I was watching the news. One particular story caught my attention.

"Come here honey, you need to see this."

A limo packed with the bride and groom and the entire wedding party: twelve souls in the limo including the chauffeur and two bystanders perished in the crash. The limo was going down a very steep hill. The chauffeur lost control and smashed into a parked SUV. The collision was so violent, the SUV rolled over several times and struck two innocent bystanders. Fourteen people died.

"Damn honey, How many times have I wished to be wrong? Especially when it comes to that type of situation."

"It's sad. In a blink of an eye, the entire wedding party is gone on their way to the wedding. I know it takes a toll on you, turn off the TV. It's enough news for today."

I turned off the television and stared at the wall for a few minutes. The day after watching the devastating news of the accident of the wedding party, when I came home from work, my wife told me earlier in the day that there was a full body apparition of a woman in the kitchen.

She pointed towards the coffee maker. She did a motion as if she was drinking a cup of coffee then vanished. While alive, she was probably a caffeine addict-- maybe she wanted a cup of coffee. A friend since high school wanted to talk to me. I went over to her place. She was able to defeat leukemia after a hard-fought battle. She was in remission for two years.

"The cancer is back."

"I am so sorry to hear that. I know why you want to talk with me. You want to know if you're going to see another Christmas, am I right?"

"I know you like the back of my hand. I know that you have some insight on what I am about to ask you."

"No need to ask, I already know. Come here, let me rest my hand on your shoulder."

I have answered that awful inquiry way too often for my liking. Individuals who are terminally ill, they know the end is near. The most important thing for them is: if they will be with their family for one more Christmas.

I always try not to show any emotions but people can tell with my facial expressions. After all, I am only human. When my friend requested for me to see her, it was the month of September.

"By the expression on your face, I do not know if I want to hear the answer."

"I am sorry."

"Don't be sorry, it's not your fault. I am the one who should apologize for putting you on the spot."

"You are not putting me on the spot, you know I will always be here for you no matter what. I always try to hide my emotion."

"Do not try to hide them, express what you feel. Do not be afraid to show your emotions, it will make things a lot easier for you. People will know that you have a good heart and really care about people by showing some emotions."

"It's not a question that you can answer with a straight face. Believe me, I tried so many times to answer with a straight face; for me it's impossible. Anyway, where were we? Yes, you will be able to celebrate another Christmas with your loved ones."

"By the look on your face, this will be my last celebration of Christmas. I will make sure to have super holidays with friends and family. I want to go with a bang."

"I hope that I am wrong. I am happy today that I was able to give you a positive answer in a bad situation. I can only tell you what I see, but things may change."

"Thank you for being honest with me. I had a pretty good idea that I would make it pass Christmas. I wanted a confirmation."

"You know, today, I answered your question with a heavy heart."

"I know. I better start to put my things in order."

"I am so sorry."

"Like I said, don't be sorry. It is not your fault. Be happy for me, I am going to a better place with no more pain and I will reunite with my mom and dad. I have something for you."

She showed me the photo of our classmates on graduation day.

"Can I ask you a favor?"

"Of course."

"First of all, do you have a photo of the bunch of monkeys and baboons of our graduation class?"

"No, I don't."

"I am giving you mine. I would like for you to make a copy of the photo. Put the photo in an eight by twelve frame and place it on top of my casket. You know how all of you mean to me."

"I know. Do not worry, it will be done. It's been years since I have seen this photo. Things were a lot simpler back then. The photo brings back a lot of memories."

I gave her a big hug with tears in my eyes.

"Don't be sad, be happy for me. I am going to be in a better place; beside, I am not gone yet. I am inviting you and your wife for Christmas dinner. We had some good times, many laughs over the years."

"We sure did."

She invited everyone in the photo for a Christmas dinner. Almost everyone in the photo were able to attend. We had a good time and you could see the sparkle in her eyes. She was savoring the moment. She passed away in February seven weeks after Christmas. I did what I promised to do.

One weekend, I was depressed. I stopped caring. I argued with my wife. Let's say, I was a miserable company to say the least. I was fit to be tied. I was in a totally different mindset. The doorbell rang. When I opened the door. One of my best buddies and his wife, which happens to be my cousin, were standing at the door.

"Come in."

My cousin gave me a big hug.

"Long time no see, cuz."

"Yes, way too long."

"We were driving around and you invaded my brain. You were on my mind for some reason. I told my hubby 'Let's go have a beer with my cousin'."

When we are together, we always have a great time. My cousin is always a barrel of laughs. After a fun evening, my buddy looked at his watch.

"Wow, it's getting late. Boy, time goes by fast when you are having fun and with good company."

"Yes, way too fast. Thanks for stopping by. It did me a lot of good."

After they went home, I looked at my wife.

"This evening with our friends, recharged my batteries."

I was once again ready to take on whatever came my way. The powers from above knew that I needed a boost of moral support. They chose the perfect couple to change the mindset that I was in. Funny how it works, sometimes you only need a spark to get your motor running again. That's why the little things in life are so precious.

They were able to do in one evening what a therapist would need a couple of sessions or even more to rectify the issues I was having. Every Sunday, I try to attend church. When I walk in the church, I get a warm, peaceful feeling. I feel relaxed from head to toe. I have a notion to permanently move in, find a little corner in the church so that I could pitch a tent. Make it my home.

I do not know if my wife would agree to move in the church corner with me. A man can always dream. The church is always packed with souls, seeking forgiveness-- some are lost, some are afraid of the beyond.

They hesitate to move forward. They remain in limbo. The church is a sanctuary for lost souls. My wife tells me I look so relax and at peace with myself. The feeling did not last very long.

Lunch time, the spirit of a little girl was in the house. She motioned that she was hungry and disappeared. After lunch, I was relaxing in my big comfortable chair, like the younger generation, would love to say '*I was chillin*'. A noise behind my chair brought me back to reality. It sounds like a person chained to a metal post, a foul smell in the corner. I shouted at the entity.

"Go take a shower for god's sake. You smell like yesterday's diapers; and what's with the noise with the chains. Did you escape from an insane asylum or something?"

The temperature plummeted enough that I was able to see my breath. The episode lasted a few minutes. I leaned back in my chair looking at the ceiling. I could see an evil face laughing. He gave me a quick look and he was gone. The entities work on weekends; they must be racking up a lot of overtime.

The black shadows often play with my mind. They do not have very much to play with, I have been called a pea brain on numerous occasions. They show themselves and they disappear only to make themselves visible in a different spot. It's like playing a cat and mouse game.

I try not to make a fuss and maybe they would stop their childish behavior. They are very persistent to the point that I get irritated. One night, constant knocking on the walls; I blew a gasket.

"Show yourself to me, you asshole!"

My wife was looking in my direction waving her arms.

"Behind you."

I turned around. I was looking at a solid entity right in front of me. He was as ugly as they come. An evil face with small horns on his forehead. He was black with red eyes. We came face to face. I was so pissed, I did not hold back. I let him have it, a big mistake. I continued my verbal attack.

"You are wasting your time. You are a chicken shit, always hiding and vanishing. You were probably a coward when you were alive; and still a coward in the afterlife."

He gave me a shove but it did not stop my verbal attack.

"Boy, you are an ugly son of a bitch. I now know why everybody in heaven are good looking; they send all the ugly ones in hell."

I surprised him by throwing holy water on him. I always keep a small bottle in my pocket. I started to recite prayers and he was looking at the cross on my neck. My wife came running from the bedroom with burning sage. He growled and disappeared. I yelled.

"I was right. You showed me your true colors by going away, you lazy coward. There is a song named *Coward of the County*, well guess what penis breath, you are the coward of the underworld. That's right, go hide under mama's skirt."

My wife raised her voice.

"That's enough. Don't you think that you are going overboard with your name calling? Do you think, he is going to take all that verbal nonsense sitting down? Let it go, please."

I then realized that I went a bit too far. I will suffer the consequences for my outburst of insults towards the entity. Father Joseph was not pleased with me about the confrontation.

"It was not a smart thing to do. Be careful! I am certain there will be repercussions. Keep an eye open. He will return."

He did come back with a vengeance. He came out of a black hole. A vortex in the living room, followed by demons coming out of the hole. My wife grabbed her cellphone, ran outside and called Father Joseph.

The entities cornered me and closing in. It was cold, I started shivering. I do not know if I was shivering because it was cold or me being scared. I was pushed and pinned to the wall. I could not move. The entity that I insulted came close to me. I spit in his face. I could feel pain in both my shoulders, and having a hard time breathing. I counted at least four entities.

All four were looking at me laughing. One by one, they put their hands on my stomach. When they removed their hands from my stomach, they started reciting some kind of ritual. When the reciting was done, again they were all looking at me. I could feel a burning sensation on my stomach. The heat got more intense, so did the pain. I closed my eyes; the pain was unbearable.

I was screaming like there was no tomorrow and if they kept on doing what they were doing, there will be no tomorrow. My wife came back in the house accompanied by Father Joseph and his assistant. They both ran towards me. Father Joseph tossed a bible at my feet. He was throwing holy water in my direction.

Father Joseph's partner came towards me with a large crucifix in one hand, spreading steam from a perforated device dangling at the end of a chain. He was pushed to the floor. He could not get back up on his feet. An invisible force was preventing him from moving. Father Joseph continued throwing holy water and reciting prayers.

He was shoved but continued praying; holding his crucifix as high as he could. After what it seemed to be an eternity, the demons along with the black hole vanished. I sat on the floor for a few minutes to catch my breath. Father Joseph said,

"You are lucky. We got here when we did. What they do is suffocate you and take your soul. Do not challenge them again. As you can see, they are very powerful."

"No need to worry, I will not be that dumb again. The angels that are supposed to help me. Where were they?"

"They were here. Without their help, it would have been a lot worse.

"That's why, when I was glued to the wall unable to move, I did see a white shadow come between me and the entities; but he was alone."

"No, he was not alone. They are never alone. They work in small groups of four or five."

I was shivering, and shaken up. I have to admit, for the first time, I feared for my life. I was terrified. Father Joseph advised me to go to the hospital to have my wounds checked by a doctor.

"I will. Goodnight and thanks again to both of you for coming to my rescue."

I was exhausted. I went straight to bed. My wife simply did not know what to say. I did not get much sleep, my shoulders and stomach hurt like crazy. In the morning, I went to the hospital. The doctor gave me a prescription for painkillers and sent me home. The doctor inquired on what caused the injuries.

"I rather not talk about it, you probably will not believe me anyway. All done. Thank you, Doctor."

From now on, I will think twice before losing my temper. I learned my lesson to not challenge the entity. I was lucky that I did not sustain serious injuries or worse. When I came back from the doctor's office, I could feel heat all around me. I called Father Joseph. He had this to say,

"The angels formed a shield of protection, just in case last night's company decides to return."

Thank god, everything was quiet. It took two weeks for my injuries to heal.

Chapter 14

It is a well known fact proven by statistics: more people die on Sunday evenings, Monday mornings, and during the holiday season. The reason is, a good percentage of workers do not like their jobs-- they have very stressful jobs and they deal with peer pressure everyday.

The stress level skyrockets the beginning of another work week. The dreaded Monday morning. The stress of the holidays also claims its fair share of souls. Alone during the holidays, lack of time to get things or shopping done, lack of money, family disputes. I do know this is true.

Unfortunately, there is always an increase of souls requesting guidance in this particular time frame. For me, when the lights blink twice, death will claim another soul in a very short period of time.

If the lights blink a second time during the day, what it means is that, I will have more than one spirit to guide to god's house. No matter the situations that brought the spirits to me, they take a piece of my heart with them.

I was waiting in line at the bank, a smartass walked in. As soon as he spots me, he came up to me wanting to know information concerning the health of his wife. I let him talk; let him say what he wanted to say.

"Are you done? I am well aware that you do not have a wife or a girlfriend. Are you trying to be a comedian today? Can you please come a little closer?"

He hesitated.

"Come on over here, I am not going to smack you. I promise, I won't bite. Come here."

He approached me with caution.

"No need to worry. If I wanted to fight, we would both be rolling on the floor by now. I can detect some abnormality in your eyes."

"You are pulling my leg. You are full of crap."

"Listen, I am not joking. I am dead serious. I never play games when it comes to what I can predict. I can see... oh my, my terrible, just terrible. What a shame."

By then, everyone in the bank stopped what they were doing so they could listen to what I had to say.

"My goodness! Do you allow me to put my hand on your shoulder so that..."

He interrupted me.

"Why?"

"Never mind."

"OK, OK. Go ahead."

"Have you been sick lately?"

"No, I am fit as a fiddle."

"Your fiddle needs repairs. When was the last time you went to see a doctor?"

"I do not remember; Maybe a few years ago."

I let him know the reason why my hand was on his shoulder.

"When I am dealing with an individual that is sick, I need to put my hand on his or her shoulder so that I can see the outcome."

A few more customers entered the bank. They were given the finger-over-the-mouth... *shshshsh* sign. Nobody wanted to miss a word.

"You're crazy. I am not sick."

"Alright, have it your way. I am done. FYI, some non-believers such as yourself told me the same thing. What you're telling me now that I was crazy and that I was on drugs."

"You're lying to me."

"They also told me that I was lying. I do not do drugs. They would not listen; too stubborn to make an appointment to go see a doctor. When they finally decided to go, it was too late. The damage was already done."

"What happened to these people?"

"What do you think? The local undertaker made some money with those folks."

"You really are serious."

"Of course, I am serious. I would not be wasting my time insisting to let me help you, otherwise, I would be on my way home. In a funny sort of way, it is a good thing that you talked to me although you were trying to be a smartass."

"Really, you think so?"

"It is not a coincidence that we are having this conversation. It was in the cards for us to meet."

"What do you mean it was in the cards?"

"It was planned and arranged for you to talk to me today."

"What do you mean it was planned?"

"Boy, for someone that does not believe, you sure are asking a lot of questions. Probably, your guardian angel set it up for you so that you would be able to talk to me."

"I do not believe in that sort of things."

"You should believe and have faith my friend. Faith can go a long way. For example: Today, you came to the bank before leaving your house. Did you feel a need to hurry and get here as soon as possible, as if someone or something pushed you to hurry up and get to the bank?"

"Nobody pushed me."

"I see. I will need to keep it simple for you to understand what I am trying to tell you. I did not mean someone physically push you. I have my work cut out to try to make you understand. I am doing this for your own good."

"Why?"

"Why? Because it is my job to help people."

"To tell you the truth, I had a sort of a weird feeling to hurry to get over here."

"There you go. I need to again put my hand on your shoulder. With all your questions, I can only recall bits and pieces; a small portion of what I was able to see."

"Ok, go for it."

"Now bear with me."

I put my hand on his shoulder. Closed my eyes for a few moments.

"What a shame."

"What's happening?"

I opened my eyes. I could see the anticipation in his eyes wanting to listen to what I had to say.

"Do you really want to know?"

"Yes. Goddammit! Get on with it. I do not have all day."

"Now. No need to get on your high horses. What I am about to reveal to you might not be pretty."

"Please. Go on."

"I am sorry to say. I am afraid that you will not see Christmas."

"You're kidding right? You're trying to get back at me for what I said earlier."

"Like I previously said, I do not mess around when it comes to the well-being of people. I saw green grass meaning it is summer, some brown grass and a little bit of snow which represents the fall season. That's it, nothing else."

"For real? It's that bad?"

"Yes, you should be worried. If I was in your shoes, I would do like the fictional character-- the flash, and I would be in the doctor's office in no time."

"What do you recommend me to do?"

"I just told you go see a doctor."

"I will make an appointment as soon as I get home."

I burst out laughing.

"What is so funny? "

"I really had you going. You were starting to sweat bullets: you took the bait, hook, line and sinker. Quite amusing. Actually, all I needed to do was to bring you in the boat. I do a lot of fishing and before today, you are the biggest sucker that I have hooked and was able to bring to the boat."

"Very funny."

"I was using only a ten-pound test line on my fishing rod. You did not show any resistance, no fight in you at all. Letting yourself be reeled to the boat; man, you just made my month."

"Shut up."

"I hope this will teach you not to try to impress people with your sarcasm. If you were trying to build an entourage, it backfired."

"I hope you are happy. I am leaving."

"The foundation was not very solid; it collapsed. Look, everyone is having a good chuckle at your expense. How do like them apples?"

A lady that was waiting in line whispered,

"Bravo! Good job. I think everybody was hooked on what you were telling the guy. You will need a bigger boat to put every one of us in your boat."

The knucklehead did not stay in line. Humiliated his tail between his legs, he exited the premises shaking his head. One of the customers waiting in line yelled,

"The idiot has left the building. Hallelujah, praise the lord. It made it for a very entertaining morning. It's the first time that I had so much fun coming to the bank. You were quick on the trigger to retaliate."

"I am used to it. He is not the first one and won't be the last one."

"I can very well understand. Good for you. Good show."

"Thank you."

"No, thank you for the entertainment."

A lady who was waiting in line looked at me.

"After all the drama that took place a few minutes ago, is it a good time for me to ask you a question?"

"Sure. No problem."

"Great. I will wait for you outside."

"I will be done in a few minutes."

She was waiting for me across the street. I walked over to her.

"I hope you can help me. I want to know if it is true that more people suffer heart attacks on Monday mornings, than any other day of the week."

"Yes. By the results of the studies that where conducted, it is true: Sunday evenings, Monday mornings are very stressful for a lot of people who dread to go back to work for the start of a new work week. The stress level goes through the roof."

"Yes. Well, that's my husband every morning."

"We all know that stress is the main culprit for high blood pressure which increases the risk of having a heart attack. It is the same for the holiday season."

"Oh really, I did not know that about the holidays. I guess it makes sense with all the stress."

"Why are you asking?"

"First of all, thank you for answering my question. My husband hates his job and also his boss, every morning when he leaves for work. I can see the tension and the stress in his face."

"That's not good."

"Yes, I know. He calls in sick at a rate of three, or four times a month. He is searching for another job but it's not always easy looking for another job. Can you try if you could be able to vision something?"

"I can try."

"Thank you, thank you, thank you. I really appreciate it."

I put my hand on her shoulder, but I could not detect a thing.

"It is very difficult for me to envision what the future holds for your husband. He is not sick at the moment. I am sorry."

"No need to apologize."

"Maybe, you should talk to your husband to go and see a doctor and to go see a psychic, that is… if you believe in psychic?"

"Yes, I do believe in psychics; and for the doctor every week, he says he is going to go."

"The psychic will probably be able to answer your questions. Here, I will give you her phone number. Call her and you will be amazed at what she has to say. I've seen her twice. She knocked it out of the park both times. Your husband should also go talk to a therapist and go see the doctor before it is too late."

"Thank you for your time and thank you for answering my questions."

"You're welcome. Take care and good luck."

One thing that is really annoying is when a person spots me talking to an individual. Right away, they assume he or she is sick or one of their sibling is sick. First thing you know, they are trotting in my direction.

"What is going on with him?"

"Nothing, we were only having a friendly chat. My discussion with an individual is always private; so go poke your nose somewhere else."

"No need to be so rude."

"The same goes for you. Is it an obligation or a quest for you to know everything that goes on in people's personal lives?"

"You need to stay informed what is going on in the municipality that you live in."

"My first impression of you is that you are the type of person that picks up dirt from everybody's lives and spread the lies like you said in your municipality know what you are; like a pie crust."

"A pie crust?"

"Yes, like a pie crust; flaky. I am tired to be hounded by pinocchios like you. Guys like you are worse than the paparazzi."

"Worst than who?"

"Never mind. Do you guys think, if someone confides in me, I am going to spill the beans? I can just imagine the rumors. Have you ever thought about the feelings the individual may have?"

"No, I really don't care about their feelings."

"Why am I not surprised? They put their trust in me to keep everything confidential. I am certainly not going to break their trust. What do you think, would it not be a better world if everyone would mind their own business? Here is some information for you."

"I'm listening."

"If I am seen talking to someone, tell them not to bother me, they will be wasting their time and maybe punched in the nose."

"And why would I do that?"

"I am not allowed to have a simple conversation with my fellow human being without being scrutinized by the public, as if people only talk to me when they need help."

"You called me Pinocchio."

"Yes. Look at the size of your nose. How many lies have you told with the size of your schnozzle? I would say quite a few. Goodbye."

He was standing there, mouth wide open and nothing to say. I have been wanting to sell my house now for quite some time. The reason for selling-- I want to downsize and move into a smaller house. My kids are all grown up and on their own. The house is now way too big for two people.

I have no takers. Some have inquired about the price, but they all say the same thing:"You have a nice looking house at a good price but it's haunted". I have specified with potential buyers that it is not the house that is haunted. It is me.

The spirits are in love with me. They cannot get enough of me. They never leave me alone. They will not stay in the house; they will follow me to my new residence. Potential buyers keep repeating the same thing.

They do not want to take a chance and have to move again due to the ghosts in the house. I tried renting the house with incentives first; two months free. The tenants will be able to see for themselves that the house is not haunted. Again, no takers.

A coworker needed a lift home. It was nighttime. On our way home, I spotted a dark figure in the middle of the road. Your first reaction is always to swerve. My friend had a puzzled look on his face.

"What was that all about?"

"Did you see someone standing in the middle of the road?"

"No, I did not see anything in the middle of the road; but when you swerved, you came very close to the river's embankment."

"Sorry about that. I am really tired. My eyes must be playing tricks on me."

"No worries."

I drove my friend home and made it home safe and sound. I sat in the car for a few minutes, then it dawned on me... it hit me like a ton of bricks. With the river so close to the road, the entity positioned himself at the right spot because of the fifty foot drop to the river. His plan was to make me swerve and end up in the river.

I cannot even drive home from work without causing me grief. I could have ended up in the river; no doubt about it. My friend could have been badly hurt or even killed. All he wanted was a drive home. Same for me, I only wanted to go home after a hard day at work. I was not a happy camper to say the least.

I did not tell my wife about the incident. I did not want her to have one more thing to worry about. When I was doing home repairs. When I was done, I stored my tools in their proper place. Some of the stuff already put away will fall on the floor for no reason. I pick it up only to land back on the floor again.

I came up with a wise solution. I now put my stuff in crates under lock and key. As we get older, we acquire wisdom. Same thing when I am helping my wife to clean the house; again, things keep falling all around me. Underhanded tactics, the entities use to frustrate me. It takes me twice the time to do what needs to be done.

A friend purchased an old house and invited me and my wife over for a drink; a very nice house and very well maintained by the previous owners. On our way home, my wife mentioned

"I could feel a presence in the house."

I replied.

"While standing at the door saying our goodbyes, I could see a spirit in front of the fireplace. I wonder if they know they have a guest in the house."

Another friend of ours told us they have a friendly ghost in the house. The house is more than hundred years old. Same time every night, they see headlights in the driveway. They hear the car door open and close, the shadow walks by the kitchen window and goes through the kitchen door, walks in the kitchen and living room, goes up the stairs and enters his bedroom.

He never bothers anyone except for one night. The son of our friend was mocking the ghost with laughter and bad jokes. That night while in bed, he was grabbed by the feet and pulled out of bed. When my friend heard the noise, she came running. Her son was getting back into bed.

"What happened?"

"I was pulled out of bed by the ghost."

"I am not surprised. I told you to stop mocking him and telling jokes at his expense, but you did not listen. Leave him alone. He does not bother anyone, we can all live under the same roof without prejudice."

That is the only time the spirit manifested. Father Joseph once told me, "Everything that I feel, premonitions, or visions, is telepathy". I was watching a hockey game at the local rink. I knew one of the players would get hurt. I told my friends number eight will get hurt. I can feel it.

Third period, he was hit from behind his head; hit the boards hard enough to have his bell rung. He needed help to get off the ice. He did not return to finish the game. One of my friends said, "why are we not surprised?". I call it a prediction or premonition. Father Joseph said, "I beg to differ. It's all part of telepathy".

We own horses. One day in the barn, I had an uneasy feeling about one of our horses; I was looking at him. I had the feeling that it was the last time that I would see him alive. Fortunately, it was not the case. But every time I would walk in the barn, I could feel something was about to happen.

Several weeks later, our beloved horse passed away. A blood cloth to the brain: the result of a kick to the head from another horse. He was only eight years old. A month later, I was hit again with an uneasy feeling; this time it was one of my friends who died— workplace accident.

He was walking on scaffolds, lost his footing and fell headfirst on the concrete floor. It never fails, it is a burden that I have to carry with me for the rest of my life.

It is taking an emotional toll on me. Going back to the topic of our horse who passed away, the owner of the ranch where we board our horses said it was the first time that a horse in her care died under those circumstances.

For me, it was all part of my ongoing bad luck. The death of our beloved horse was very hard for my wife to accept that he was gone. Even today, her eyes fill with tears when talking about the passing of her dear beloved horse, my wife with tears in her eyes.

"Do you know if we will be plagued with bad luck for the rest of our lives? It's getting annoying."

"I don't know. I sincerely hope not."

"It's ridiculous."

"I know."

We have been involved in several car accidents; not counting the three unfortunate deers that we hit. One of the deers that I hit was a big boy, completely demolished the car.

Constant problems with car engines, transmissions, bad luck at home. I hope when I finish paying my karmic debt, hopefully the black cloud over our heads will disintegrate into a million pieces, but it remains to be seen.

My wife was cleaning the carrying case that we use to bring the items to groom our horses. It was an emotional task for my wife; most of the items in the case were for our horse who passed away. I volunteered to clean the case for her.

"Thank you for wanting to clean the case for me, but I need to clean it to be able to have closure."

Underneath one of the bottles, my wife found a pendant made of copper the size of a quarter. On the pendant, the virgin Mary is holding baby Jesus in her arms. We have no idea how the pendant made its way in the case. The owners and the staff at the ranch all confirmed they never seen that pendant before.

We cannot find an explanation or reason why it was in the grooming case. When we are done grooming the horses, we always bring the case home. We store the case in the basement, lock it in a trunk to prevent the cats and our dog to put their paws on the items and make a mess. My wife thoroughly cleaned the pendant. It looks great.

We stored the pendant in a safe place to make sure not to lose or have it stolen; it is an incredible find to say the least. The significance as to why the pendant ended up among our grooming tools is still a mystery. This is one for the books I can tell you that much; one of our unsolved mysteries. We hope someday we will have our answer that we are looking for.

There is a saying, *With patience comes great rewards*. I hope so. Father Joseph is guessing that it could be an omen or a message of some sort that I am supposed to decipher. Father Joseph was baffled.

"To tell you the truth, I am not sure. It is very strange for your wife to have found the pendant."

"We empty the carrying case; quite often to clean it. It's weird that the pendant was found after our horse died. I wish, whoever is responsible for us to find the pendant, could have scribbled a few words on a piece of paper and leave the note next to the pendant."

"If it was only that easy, I am baffled with this one. You bring me news or items that I cannot comprehend why it's happening. One day, my brain will bust wide open if you keep confusing me; why these events are occurring."

"You're confused, but not as much as I am."

"I cannot find any information in books concerning the topics you bring. My superiors and I were having a lot of difficulty finding answers for you. I think we should write a book about you. It would make the best sellers list in no time."

"If you share the moolah, I have no objections."

"A lot of strange things and events in this world that we cannot explain. Give me the pendant for a moment, I am going to bless and dip it in holy water. Keep it in a safe place."

"Don't you worry, we already found the perfect location. Once again, thank you for your time."

One evening getting out of my truck, I noticed a flash of light in the sky. I looked up at the sky-- no upcoming storm, no thunder, no lightning in the vicinity. Nothing came to mind as to why the sky lit up like that; then I spotted two white shadows shaped like angels warning me to be careful because of the black entities in the house. When I walked in, my wife met me at the door.

"I can sense an evil presence."

"Again, dear lord, I cannot have a moment of peace and quiet in my own home. What am I supposed to do? So far, we have tried everything under the sun and then some to get rid of these annoying pest."

The dog was barking at something we could not see. I was able to calm him down, but he was still looking in one direction. I was in the kitchen while my wife in the living room. We both heard a noise. My wife inquired,

"Honey, is it you that is responsible for the noise?"

"No."

The noise was like a person shuffling a big pile of papers. The shuffling noise, lasted close to an hour before it finally stopped. I made a joke about the disturbance. The entity did not have a good filing system; it took him one hour to find one document.

"Get with the program and don't be so stingy. The age of technology is upon us. Get yourself a computer, you lousy cheapskate! "

There was some growling-- a flash of cold air.

"I must have insulted him with my comments."

Later that night, we were preparing to go to snooze land when my wife looked at the window.

"I can see the face of a native man in the bedroom window, looking at you."

"For some strange reason, I am unable to see him."

After a few minutes, my wife mentioned.

"He is gone."

I wonder what or why he was staring at me through the bedroom window: ghosts, spirits,or angels, might be trying to send me signals, or messages. I still have no clue what to make of it.

I often rev up the motor in my brain. I even put it in overdrive to try to make sense-- meanings of certain apparitions, signals, certain gestures. It's driving me up to wall to not understand.

Maybe if I had a bigger brain, I might be able to decipher some of the stuff they keep sending me. My brain only has a v4 engine. I might trade it in for a v8, that way I might be able to make sense of what I am supposed to understand.

I will start looking if I can find some sort of ghost college to take classes on the subject of dealing with messages and signals so they can be as easy as 1 2 3… to understand their meaning. No more hitting my head on walls for me to try to understand. It is driving me nuts not knowing.

When I was a kid, I was so bright that my dad called me sun. All kidding aside, if I would be able to know what they mean, it would certainly give me an edge… better prepared when I face off against the dark side. I would have a lot less battle scars and emotional stress.

One night, we were both sound asleep. The clock radio on the night table beside the bed began blaring a very loud music. We almost fell out of bed. Boy, what a rude awakening! I said to my wife.

"Before falling asleep, did you play with the radio like maybe setting the right time or something?"

"No."

The dog was barking while looking towards the hallway. I got up, took a peek in the hallway only to find one of our cats mortally wounded and the other cat severely injured. The cats were full of blood. I was looking at the face of the deceased cat.

I saw the face of a smiling devil; it all made sense. The loud music was to cover the noise of the cats being brutalized. I will not write the words that came out of my mouth, it would be inappropriate reading. The book would be rated R.

We took both cats to the vet. The severely injured cat was too badly hurt to recuperate from his wounds. It was like he was crushed by something. We had no choice but to put him down.

The vet came to the conclusion that our deceased cat died as a result of a massive blow to the head. Killing our cats was a low down underhanded trick-- like being hit below the belt. The black entities have no scruples whatsoever. No regards for the living. The killing of the cats was another massive emotional blow for my wife.

We buried both cats in our backyard so they can rest in peace. A total of four cats now who perished, succumb due to injuries. We decided no more felines in the house. It is too painful when they die. The entities will no longer have cats to torment and eventually kill them. We are keeping a close eye on our dog, with all the turmoil at home with animals and entities.

I threw away my nice hat for a grumpy hat. I had an outburst of anger, talking trash. All that was coming out of my mouth was profanity. After half an hour of ranting raving like a lunatic, I was finally able to get off my high horse. I calmed down, I did not do myself any favors by emptying my basket of frustrations in such an offensive language.

Once again, I prayed for forgiveness from the powers above. I was outside in my yard, my neighbors porch light blinked twice. The sky lit up with no storms on the horizon. I know my siblings that passed are angels. I am aware they help me, but I often wonder, could they make more efforts to take that extra step that I often need to get me out of the woods?

Where were they when our cats were attacked? Did they help me or, were they observing from a distance? One thing, they were quick to respond when I needed to be forgiven for my foolish behavior.

Father Joseph once told me they do help; but sometimes the enemy is too strong-- the devil. The dark angels are a formidable adversary; do not expect miracles, you will be greatly disappointed. My wife was still upset with me because of my outburst of profanity.

"It's a good thing the cops were not patrolling in our neighborhood. They would have taken you for a ride in the paddy wagon. Your attire for the evening would have been a straight jacket."

"That bad."

"Yes, that bad. If you ever take another tantrum like that again, I will have it on video and invite all your friends over for a beer so they can enjoy watching their friend making a fool of himself."

My wife's best friend resides four hundred kilometers away. She called my wife to let her know that her mom was diagnosed with cancer. I answered the phone. We talked a few minutes about the prognosis of her mother before handing the phone over to my wife.

I went into another room to give my wife some privacy. When the call ended, my wife rejoined me in the living room. I had to break the bad news to my wife. The mother of her friend will not make it. My wife was surprised that I could predict the outcome from such a distance.

"I hope you are wrong."

"So do I."

"I am surprised you can tell that far."

"I know, but for her mother, I had an overwhelming feeling and I do not know why?"

Unfortunately, I was right. The poor lady died seven months after the diagnosis that she was suffering from lung cancer. I am still baffled that I can predict a outcome from so far away and sometimes I am only a few feet away from someone and I cannot see anything. Father Joseph could not find the reason for my dilemma.

I was having another rough day. I blew my top again. In the evening, I was still steamed. I decided to go to bed early. I did not want to deal with the continuous bad luck; everyday bullshit from the public.

When I went to bed, I was still fuming over an event that took place in the morning. I could not sleep, I was staring at the ceiling. That day for some unknown reason, I had a hard time to put my feet back on the ground. I do not know why, I was having such difficulty of letting go of the hiccups of the day. Usually when I get upset, an hour at the most, I have regained my senses.

I was tossing, turning, getting even more frustrated due to the fact I was not able to sleep. Like taxes, my temperature was rising again. I was about to bust the frustration thermometer. I was facing the bedroom window and I could see flashing lights. I got out of bed to take a look. The cops pulled over a car, a coincidence, I think not. The reason why it is not a coincidence, the cops pulled over a car.

Behind my house, there is a small field-- a road at the end of the field with a very small volume of traffic. I estimate maybe ten to fifteen cars a day use the road to get to their destination. I have been living in my house for many years. The cops rarely patrol the road due to the lack of traffic. What are the odds? They would pull over a car. Especially, when I decide to hit the sack early.

Looking at the lights brought me back to earth. I was able to see an angel looking at me. I knew it was a message from my guardian angel and his associates for me to get a grip of myself and calm down. My patience is slowly dwindling which is not a good thing.

People ask me why the lights, instead of another method to relay messages. I do not know why. I guess, for the angels, it is the convenient way to contact me. To tell you the truth, I really don't know.

We decided to get another dog. For some strange reason, the entities left my dog alone. We purchased a wolfdog puppy. It was urgent that we contact the individual that will bring our little puppy home. We called a few times and left messages. There was no return call. My wife was worried.

"I do not like to be in limbo."

"No need to worry. I have a hunch that I will have contact with him today."

After lunch, I was at the supermarket and there he was. I walked over to him.

"We have been trying to reach you."

"I was out of town."

"We left a few messages."

"I have not been to the house yet. This is my first stop to buy a bit of groceries, so I won't have to go back out when I get home."

We discussed the arrangements for the delivery of our new pet. I gave my wife the good news.

"I was right this morning that I was going to see him today. My hunches, they never let me down. Our puppy will be home tomorrow."

"Tomorrow? That's great."

"When I was backing up to exit the parking lot of the store, a black entity was standing behind the truck. I did not stop and when I was too close for his liking, he dissolved into tiny black orbs."

That same night, I was in the kitchen looking out the window. The porch light from one of my neighbors came on. I was able to see a white shadow enter into the neighbor's house. And for us for a change, we enjoyed a peaceful evening. The next morning, I was shaving and the doors of the medicine cabinet opened and closed by themselves.

"Whoever it is, cut it out."

I was pushed from behind.

"OK, you had your fun. Please leave me alone so that I can finish shaving."

A gust of cold air, the entity was gone. I was able to finish shaving with no further interruptions. It is ridiculous being annoyed by a pest while shaving. Maybe he wanted to borrow my electric razor.

My wife organized a surprise birthday party for me. She invited a bunch of my friends-- a nice little gathering. While having dinner, my wife took pictures. I looked at some of the pictures. I was surrounded by spirits.

My friends all took turns looking at the photos. They were all dumbfounded at what they saw and with the amount of spirits around me. One of my friends took the time to count how many there was.

"I counted nine different spirits."

"Let's forget about the photos and get this party going. Let's shake this place off its foundation."

We had a blast. A few weeks later, we were spending a weekend with friends at their cottage. With the reflection of a full moon and slight breeze, you could see floating diamonds on the lake. A gorgeous night to say the least. My wife decided to take photos of the gorgeous scenery.

We made our way to the lake. My wife took photos of me standing on the dock next to my friend's pontoon boat. She also took photos of the dancing diamonds on the lake and shining in the moonlight. We looked at the photos. You could clearly see white shadows floating next to me. In the morning, I showed my friend the photos that were taken the night before.

"Tell me what you see."

When he was done, he looked at me.

"They follow you everywhere."

"Yes, I carry them in my back pocket. They are my bodyguards."

We were in the middle of a heat wave you could fry an egg on the hood of my truck. I was not able to sleep. I was sweating like a politician under oath. I was sitting on the couch facing the patio doors.

I could see lightning and hear the thunder coming over the mountains and over the lake. The storm was heading our way. Good that it might put an end to the scorching temperature. As the storm got closer, I was looking at the lightning.

I could not believe my eyes. There it was-- the face of satan in one of the lightning bolts. He wanted to let me know not to get too comfortable; that he was never far away.

He is actually keeping tabs on me... incredible, it was a long weekend. Two more days before we go home. I hope he leaves me alone. We were able to enjoy the remaining of the weekend without a glitch. When we came home from our weekend trip, before opening the door, I could hear some noise. I looked at my wife.

"Do you hear that?"

"Yes."

When I opened the door, we could hear a loud noise: It was a new ballad. When we hear new grinding music, we call it a ballad. It was not easy to describe. It was like a metallic noise, like steel grinding on steel.

We were still standing in the doorway, trying to determine what the heck we were dealing with. I took one step to enter in the house.

It was over no more noise. The dogs were barking at Mr. Invisible and wanting to enter the house.

A little later in the afternoon, the noise made a triumphant return. I was unable to find the source or the origin of that awful nerve racking noise. The dogs were barking. I was able to convince myself not to lose my cool. We stepped outside along with the dogs in tow. My blood pressure was boiling again, but I remained calm.

My neighbor came over and inquired about the racket.

"Do you have someone in the house that is using sandpaper on cans?"

"No and to tell you the truth, I have no clue."

My neighbor looked at me.

"You have no clue where the racket comes from in your house?"

With a puzzled face, my neighbor looked at me.

"I am truly sorry. We just got here from a weekend at my friend's cottage. I will get to the source of this insane noise."

"OK, but try to keep it down."

"I will do my very best to get rid of that nuisance."

My neighbor walked away shaking his head. We closed all the windows in the house to minimize the noise. Finally after ten minutes, the noise stopped. The silence was music to our ears. At one point, the noise was so loud. I am convinced that a deaf person would have been able to hear the noise. I said to my wife,

"You know what honey, I was refreshed, relaxed and in a good mood after spending the weekend with our friends but look at me now. I am steaming, you could boil eggs on my forehead but I did not blow my top."

"I am proud of you, kudos to you sweetheart."

"Thank you. I appreciate that."

In the evening when we were watching television, two drops of water dripped on my head. I was drawn to the window. I called my wife over.

"You need to see this."

My wife was now looking out the window.

"Can you see what I see?"

"Yes, I see a blue color shaped like a cross radiating from the porch light of our neighbor."

The next day, I called my fountain of knowledge to let him know that I was on my way to see him. When I arrived, I gave him all the information regarding the blue cross. Father Joseph specified. This was not a first for him.

"I've had a few inquiries before yours today. The angels dropped holy water on your head; the cross was a message not to lose faith. The entities know that you are struggling right now with your temperament, which brings negativity in the house. They are stronger. They are gaining some momentum. The ball is in their court my friend, they will use it."

"Boy, OK. I was not inspecting that kind of response but OK."

"I hate to admit it they now have an edge on you; you will need to shape up or ship out. They know they are now getting to you with very little manifesting."

"How do they know that I am getting weaker when it comes to my patience? Do they have one of their colleagues on the sidelines taking notes or something?"

"They are getting to you. They found your weakness. They will be relentless to put you down and make sure that you are too weak to get back up. They will have full control over you. They will celebrate and have a victory parade. At all cost, you cannot let the dark side win."

"Back up the truck for a minute; you said at all costs. This is not like in a war, the general gives you the order to hold a bridge at all cost. I am certainly not going to give my life for the things that I do."

"Never mind, you missed the point."

"Father, do you know this is the second episode with holy water on my head? Do you recall when I mentioned the rain drops on my head? The clouds shaped like angels."

"Yes, I do recall having the conversation with you about the rain drops and the angels, what you need to do now is to dig deeper into your soul. Get your hands dirty and give them what they deserve, make them pay for what they are doing."

When we were done talking, I was walking to my truck. There was a flash of light in my hands. I went back in, to tell Father Joseph about the light in my hand.

"I cannot educate you on that one. I don't even know myself the meaning with the flash of light. You never cease to amaze me."

That night, I did a lot of soul searching. Father Joseph was right: all hands on deck. I will do whatever it takes. I took a shower. When I was done, I could see yellow eyes in the bathroom window.

"Well, what do you know they also have peeping toms working for them. How disgusting! How low can they go?"

I noticed strange symbols written on the wall. The bathroom light flickered a few times. The face of the devil was on the bathroom door and also on the ceramic tiles on the floor. I do not want to gross people out but I urinated on the tile that was showing the face of the devil.

"Now you know what I think of you, airhead."

When I entered my bedroom, the lamp on the night table gave me a light show.

"Look honey, I am back in the late seventies or early eighties. Get down baby. it's disco time."

When I came back from memory lane, the lamp was on the floor followed by a big bang on the wall. My wife was standing in front of the window.

"It is getting cold. I can feel cold air around me."

A black entity exited the room through the window. My wife opened the window and looked outside. She saw a crow on the ledge of the gazebo. A coincidence, maybe, I don't know. I still have no idea why there was a crow on the ledge and I still don't know the reason for the flash of light in my hands.

Father Joseph did warn me that the paranormal would escalate. He hit the nail on the head with that one. It hit me like a bolt of lightning. I now know the reason why we always feel a breeze when the entities make their presence known. They are a bunch of airheads. Why did I not think about that one sooner is beyond me?

It took a lot of effort on my part to not lose my marbles again, but unfortunately, I could not refrain myself; all hell broke loose. I argued with some of my friends, my wife, and I tossed some furniture around. I was exactly where I did not want to be, I was arguing with my wife. We both noticed a white mist that floated between us. My wife looked at me.

"That's my grandmother. She joined us for us to end our argument."

My wife was still looking at me with a puzzled look on her face.

"Why are you looking at me with that look on your face?"

"I again saw my grandfather through you."

"Strange, I was not aware of his presence. I should have been able to notice the change taking place even if it's only a few seconds. I did not feel a thing… very strange indeed. Are you certain that your…"

She interrupted me.

"Yes, I did."

"OK, OK, I believe you, but I cannot understand that I was not aware when he manifested through me. Oh well, another one for the books."

We both apologized to each other. It was quiet in the house.

"Let's make some popcorn and watch a film."

I parked my carcass on the couch next to my better half. My hair was pulled, laughter was coming from behind the couch. I turned around and a black entity looked at me and vanished.

"Same hold, same hold. The buggers, they hit and run."

After the movie was over, we made our way to the bedroom. In one of the corner of the room, spirits were shining like stars on a clear night; angels commenced singing. They looked at us with a big grin for about a minute and vanished. There was a peaceful ambiance and a fragrance of lavender in the entire house. We slept like babies.

The next morning, I was on my way out to go and apologize to the people I offended with my outburst of anger. I came face to face with a black angel. I did not even flinch; I kept on walking. He disappeared. In our driveway, a full body apparition of a women dressed in army fatigues. From what I observed, she was crying. She pointed towards the sky. I nodded yes.

I closed my eyes. I was in a trance until her soul was in heaven. Forty five minutes from home is the location of a large army base. That night watching the news, a reporter was referring to a morning accident on the base-- a female soldier was killed in a training accident.

At a New Year's Eve party, I was having a great time-- good music, good friends, good food, the whole nine yards. When a friend of a friend introduced herself,

"My name is Linda. I can see ghosts and spirits but I cannot make predictions."

"I know all the information pertaining what a sensitive can do. My wife is a sensitive."

"That's good. I can feel a presence-- an entity with red eyes."

"My wife said the same thing. I can see red eyes in the window after a few seconds, and the eyes are gone."

I introduced my wife. I said to both of them,

"Yes, I did notice the red eyes in the window but no offense, you are a kind and polite person but I am not at this gathering to talk about ghost and goblins. That goes for you too, honey."

"No offense taken, I understand. I will not say a word."

"One question, who told you about me?"

"Your friend, Roger."

She rejoined her friends.

The entity was still present in the room. I did not want to jinx the party, I kept my mouth shut and so did Linda. She kept her word. She did not whisper a word about what we discussed. After a few minutes, I could no longer see the entity. I presumed that he was gone.

When the time came to go home, I used the remote starter to start the car. The entity was sitting in the front seat of the car. When we reached the car, the entity was gone. He must have hitched a ride with one of the guest at the party. On our way to the car, I let my wife know that I was cold most of the evening.

"Why did you not say a word that you were cold?"

"Although being cold, I was having a great time. I really let loose tonight."

"Yes, I know and good for you, it's going to do the body good."

"Yes, I needed an evening like tonight. The coke bottle that was on the table for most of the evening, I picked it up and threw it in the garbage. The bottle was still freezing cold. Everyone around me were using ice cubes except me. Were you cold when you were by my side?"

"No, but the entity paid you a few visit."

"Really, I did not notice. That's why I was cold for the whole evening. He made sure that I was unable to see him or else I would have offered him a beer."

My wife drove home. I indulged a little too much in the liquid spirits. A few days later, I was thinking of my friend who owns a landscaping company. During the winter season, he does snow removal. I was about to contact him when my wife inquired.

"At what time is your friend coming to plow the driveway?"

You call that"telepathy". I did not say a word to her that I was about to contact him and hire his company to keep our driveway plowed all winter.

A good majority of the population are convinced, animals have no souls. I am not so sure about that. I see the ghost of my dearly departed dog from years ago; we were a team. Next to my wife, he was my best friend. The answer for one particular question is: No, I do not guide dead animals to heaven.

One day while doing errands, I ran into a neighbor that used to live across the street from me. I had not seen him since he moved several years ago; although the age gap between us, we built a good friendship as neighbors. We talked for a little while. When he said goodbye, I knew it was the last time I would see him alive. Fifteen days later, he died of a heart attack. He was ninety- two years old.

He was a decorated World War II veteran. I guided his soul to heaven. It was meant for us to run into each other that day, his spirit was making preparations in advance. He made sure for me to see my old friend before he passed in order for me to guide his spirit to climb the stairs to heaven; like the seventies song, *Stairways to Heaven*.

While we were on the topic of music, I was in my living room listening to music when I noticed a human face with tears in her eyes. Another lost soul that needed guidance. I did what I needed to do.

One morning, at the foot of our bed, a female spirit reeking of perfume was staring at us. My wife inquired if there was something she could do for her. She walked out of the room and vanished, another spirit just passing through. That morning while outside, I could hear a very faint male voice trying to talk to me.

"Can you please repeat what you said, so that I can understand what you are trying to tell me."

Nothing but silence. I waited a few more minutes and still nothing; another intriguing event with no answers.

That night, same faint voice from earlier in the day, but this time he whistled in my ears for two hours, preventing me from sleeping. I can only guess while scavenging earlier in the day, he was able to put his hand on a whistle. Again, I was aggravated for not being able to sleep.

Chapter 15

Going back to the New Year's Eve party that I attended; that night I consumed my fair share of booze. I said to my wife,

"You know honey, the other night at the party, the more I was downing drinks, the less I cared about everything. It was a good feeling: no worries, no stress."

"What are you trying to say... that the booze is the answer to all your problems?"

"Yes, and I am going to the liquor store."

The New Year's party was the trigger that started my drinking problem and I started drinking more and more.

My drinking binge was for a period of about six months. One morning, I woke up with an enormous hangover. I was sure my head was going to explode. I do not know how many aspirins went down my throat that day; probably close to a full bottle. That was my wake up call. I looked at myself in the mirror and boy oh boy, I did not like what was standing in front of the mirror.

"Man, oh man what a disgrace and shameful lunatic behavior. What was I thinking? What a mess. What the hell am I doing? Have I turned into a chicken shit, hiding behind a bottle of booze?"

I was really ashamed of myself like you would not believe and I needed to fix the problem, not tomorrow or the day after tomorrow, but today. My drinking was causing mayhem for the ones close to me. The more serious victim is my wife. She was nervous when I was not home. She started sleepwalking looking for me; that is how worried she was.

In the daytime, she was walking on pins and needles. Every time I went to bed, (that was if I could reach my bed), I fall asleep and not wake up; or fall and injure myself.

I was feeling no pain. I was driving under the influence. I was blessed for not causing an accident or killing innocent victims. Pulled over by the cops and lost my license; that would have been awkward for me not to drive. My family was ready to disown me. I was no longer on speaking terms with Father Joseph. The black entities did not bother with me anymore; I was no longer a threat.

Many spirits were in limbo until they could find their own way to the gates of heaven. The souls had to fend for themselves with entities that were causing them grief, trying to prevent them from joining god. Some did not make it, they were snatched by black entities and brought to hell for eternity.

People would say, '*Look at him! Not only does he take drugs, he is drunk again*'. They assumed I was taking drugs while drinking. I have no shame. I stopped cold turkey and never looked back. You should not look back; your future is ahead of you.

Every morning you have two choices: continue to sleep with your dreams or wake up and chase them. Dreams never die just the dreamer. It feels great to be sober again, back on track. I apologized to everybody. I started reciting prayers to god for forgiveness. I made peace with Father Joseph.

I always said, life is like a boxing ring. Everytime you take a punch that sends you to the canvas, get right back up and face your opponent. If you stay down, the fight is over. I did not even listen to myself. I have been sober since the morning with the humongous hangover. I will never go down that trail again. I put up barriers and blocked the trail. No more access to foolishness.

My wife does not walk in her sleep anymore. I say thank you to my wife every day for her patience with me. She appreciates the fact that I say thank you every day which she says it is not necessary; but she did let me know that for a while, I was walking on thin ice. Things have not changed. We were attending a wedding when some nut grabbed the microphone.

"We have a ghost hunter among us tonight."

"Here we go again."

The blabbermouth handed the microphone to the master of ceremony. She was looking at me.

"Come on up. I want to know if I am going to live a long and healthy life."

"The answer is no if she does not close that hole in her face."

Some of the guests were giggling, talking among themselves. One individual got up, yelled out loud,

"There is no such thing as ghosts, it is all make-believe. Because when you die, the curtain and the lights go down for the last time."

He was not looking at me while he was talking. He continued by saying,

"You're making a mountain of money by telling everyone that their houses are haunted."

The bride and groom came to my rescue. The groom took the microphone.

"Let's clear the air and everybody listen. He is not a ghost hunter; you guys do not even know him. If you did, you would leave him alone. He is here tonight by invitation like the rest of you. He was kind enough to attend our wedding. They are here today to have a good time like every one of you."

He was looking at everybody in the hall.

"If I hear one word of profanity aimed at him, I will personally escort you to the door. Capeesh? Your rowdy behavior has already put a damper on the evening. For those who want to know, he is my beloved cousin. That's right, ladies and gentlemen; he is my favorite cousin. As cousins, we are close like two peas in the same pod."

Later in the evening, a guest suffered a heart attack. I rushed over, he was unresponsive. I was able to resuscitate him. The ambulance arrived. He was whisked away to the hospital. The groom again takes the microphone.

"What do you think of him now?"

Some guest shook my hand, some applauded. We celebrated a little longer than expected. We went home in the wee hours of the morning. The heart attack victim made a full recovery, which I new he would, not because I am the one who immediately jumped into action and performed CPR. I just knew. One of my brother's co-worker inquired,

"If I go see your brother, will he be able to give me an idea when I will kick the old bucket?"

"No."

"How come he is the only one in your family with special powers?"

"What makes you think that he is the only one?"

"I know that he is the weirdo of your family. Who died and made him king? Does he think that he is god or something? What makes him better than us?"

My brother remembered what I told him to always say yes. It does not matter what the nature of the question is, or comments that are thrown your way. Just keep saying yes. If you do, they might stop bothering you. My brother replied yes to all his questions. His final answer was,

"Go ask him yourself. I am sure, he will be more than happy to answer your dumb questions."

"Some help you are."

My brother started singing,

"Que sera, sera. Whatever will be will be, que sera sera."

The singing put an end to his questions. My wife is also constantly dealing with the same questions.

"Do you see what your husband is able to see?"

Her response is always the same,

"To a certain extent, yes. When it comes to guiding souls to heaven, that I cannot see. "

Some individuals want to know why I am not willing to be interviewed, either on the radio or television. I have all kind of excuses thrown my way: afraid they will find out I am a fake, making money under the table, etc. My new response for these questions.

"Go see Mr. Lamp, he might be able to shed some light on the matter. You make sure to go see Mr. Lamp, because if you see Mr. Knight he is going to keep you in the dark."

With that type of response, I know all the cuss words that are out there. Some dumb individual asked who is Mr. Lamp. A lot of people say, I do it for glory. Boy, they missed the bullseye on that one. I do what I am supposed to do on this god forgiving earth.

Many think that someday, I will have my own television show. For that to materialize is like the same thing as the Pillsbury doughboy surviving a baking convention. Inquiries if I keep records of the events?

"Yes. Here, I will give you the key to my office, you morons."

It's not like I would be the owner of a company or even a doctor to keep files in a filing cabinet. I have an impeccable memory; my records are filed between my ears. I took advantage of that empty space to keep my records.

Do I believe in prophecies? Do I get to read from the book of prophecies and the book of Nostradamus?

I always reply,

"None of your business."

I wonder if it is me that is not very good at relaying information or, people do not listen and understand the meaning of leaving me alone. Over the years, individuals with disabilities have come to me if I could cure their disabilities. Sometimes, I am a bit rude with them.

I hate myself for doing that; I am sure if I was in their shoes, I would do the same. Too bad, I do not have a magic pill to give them. I am not a faith healer. I cannot perform miracles. I cannot walk on water. A paraplegic was upset with me because I could not do anything for him.

"Word on the street is that you help certain individuals with disabilities. Did I not meet your criteria? Why won't you help me? Is it because I do not have any money?"

"It's none of that, I simply cannot do it. I do not know who you were speaking with, he or she was way off base with his or her information. The talk about me are only rumors or lies. No offense but you should get your facts straight before charging full speed ahead to see me."

He kept looking at me with darts in his eyes.

"That way, you will not get your hopes up and the agony of getting a no for an answer. I know that you are not happy with me but, can you do me a favor? Please pass the word to not come to see me with high expectations and for me to take the wind out of their sails when I tell them that I cannot help them. Please, can you do that for me?"

"And why should I do that. You're not willing to help me so why should I help you?

"You have no idea how I detest the situations when I have to deflate your balloons. I feel for you, please believe me I really do. I am truly sorry. Please believe me when I say this: In my family, we also have disabilities of our own. So, I know where you're coming from."

"You're right, we always presume before hearing the full story."

We shook hands and he was on his way. A ton of curious people want to know how can I go from one dimension to another. My response is always the same: only when I am ready to go to sleep.

While snoring, which my wife says my snoring is loud enough to bring the house down, I travel to different dimensions. My wife has said to me on several occasions that it is kind of freaky. My head is on my pillow and my eyes are wide open. She can tell when I am back in my bed; I close my eyes.

In some dimensions, I am very privileged to be surrounded by angels; the other dimensions have gorgeous landscapes. I also see the dark side which is home for black angels, and entities.

The dark side is full of souls wanting to leave but they are trapped. They are there for a reason. As a matter of fact, I do not know if there is a way to get trapped souls out of the dark side. A colleague of Father Joseph once advised me that an empty landscape means a lot of uncertainties in this world.

My biggest critic is my monster inlaw, oops, I mean my mother in law. She is a non believer. Every time we visit, she says that I should be ashamed with my lies and made-up stories to swindle unsuspecting people. I have reiterated the same thing more than once.

"I know you do not believe in that kind of stuff, but can you please keep your unwanted opinions to yourself? I would have gotten better results if I was talking to the wall. If I lie to people like you say, don't you think I would always have negative feedback?"

"How do I know that you do not get negative feedback when I am not there to listen?"

"No, angry people want to beat me up."

"That's what you need: someone to rattle your cage."

"Would people be dumb enough to keep in contact with me? Or ask for my help?"

"You brainwash them."

"My, my, my, you're searching in the bottom of the barrel for your replies. You mean to tell me, I cannot do what I am supposed to do but I have the power to brainwash people. Interesting. I certainly do not need to explain myself to you."

She is my wife's step-monster. The day we were introduced, I knew right away we would not get along. The air in her apartment is still polluted with her attitude towards me. I do not care; I can live with that.

When attending a funeral, I observe the spirits. The loved ones that have passed, angels over the coffin or urn. When the funeral comes to an end, the angels or spirits make their way back to paradise. I can tell they are at peace. I cannot attend a funeral without someone bugging me for something.

"What do you see when you are in church attending a funeral?"

"What I see is very simple to answer. I see the same things that you see."

"You don't see anything else?"

I simply walk away without answering the question. I do not want to open a can of worms and answer questions all day long. The one thing that I have a hard time to cope with, is the spirit of a baby. I am drawn to their spirits like a magnet. I know they are confused and lost. I always wonder, 'why so young?'. They were not given a chance to enjoy the life ahead of them.

We are all born innocent and we all die guilty of something. The poor babies are innocent when they pass away. They did not have enough time on this earth to be guilty of committing a sin. I am not one to judge but like I said, it makes me wonder why so young.

There must be a reason. I need to take extra precautions while guiding their soul to heaven. The dark side is always on the watch if the entities try to snatch their souls and bring the poor innocent souls to hell.

They are the perfect souls for the dark angels to manipulate. The spirits or souls do not know any better; they are too young to understand. All they will ever know is the scorching heat of hell.

My wife can tell when I help a young soul. I always shed a few tears. My hands are joined together. I was having tremendous problems guiding and communicating with the spirits. The entities found a way to block signals. I did not know the reason about the difficulty of doing my job.

I was confused; the souls were confused or lost. The dark side was able to collect a few souls before I was able to rectify the problem. I needed the help of a priest. Again, I knocked on Father Joseph's door. He was not available to help me; one of his associates agreed to give me a helping hand. I did not know what to expect. He was new to our parish.

"For this problem, we need to be in the church."

"Lead the way, Father."

It did not take him long to detect the problem: A circle of entities around me. They were interfering by not letting the spirits reach me.

"I do not understand how I was not able to detect the interference myself."

"They are very sneaky culprits; they are well aware that if they get too close ,you will put a dent in their plans that is why they maneuver from a safe distance. They are slick, that's for sure."

We did the circle of lights. A circle of burning candles with me in the middle of the circle. I walked in the circle by spraying incense, along with prayers. The priest was walking around outside the circle, with a cross and a bible in his hands chanting prayers. The spirits finally vanished and the barrier around me was no more.

"They are gone the fence around you collapsed. You need to understand that some entities will never make themselves known."

"You were able to see them?"

"When you stepped into the church, they became restless. I was able to detect some movement. Keep a blessed bible close at hand. Make sure that the bible is not out of reach at all times; very critical that you do so. If you feel something suspicious or something that is not right, lift the bible over your head and pray out loud. It might not resolve the issue but it would be a start."

"Thanks, but I already have one."

"Two is better than one. Keep one in your pocket and the other one at home."

He blessed the mini bible.

"Here, put the bible in your pocket. Always make sure that the bible follows you everywhere you go."

"Thank you. I am impressed with your knowledge and grateful for all your work. If it was not for you, I would still be scratching my head to come up with effective techniques to keep them at bay. Thanks again."

"You're welcome. Be vigilant. Try to sleep with one eye open."

I received a letter from a lunatic. Here is the content of the letter: *'If you do not give me the stash of money that you scammed from the population, I will reveal to the public that you are a professional scam artist'.*

Apparently, he had proof. The letter also included instructions with a time and place to meet and not to tell anyone because if I do, all he needs to do is press a key on his laptop, and the information will be on the internet in a matter of seconds.

"If you know what I am saying, bring the loot as requested and everything will be fine".

I almost burst my ribs from laughter.

"This bozo is hilarious."

The numbnut sent the letter with a return address. The address was from a neighboring town. I put money from the Monopoly game in an envelope. I wrote a letter asking him if he was on a weekend pass from the insane asylum. If not, that is where this pinhead belongs. Does he realize his address is on the envelope?

He is watching too much television. He is lucky that I am a nice guy because the letter would be in the hands of the authorities that he is trying to blackmail me. If he does that again, I will not be so nice. Funny, there is no second letter. I wonder why.

When you confront evil entities, you never know what to expect. One thing is for sure: it is never pleasant. Some come back to get a second chance to redeem themselves, be forgiven for their sins, while some are frustrated. They cannot stand where they are. They take their frustration on the living.

I keep reminding them. They had a choice in life: be good or be bad. *'If you chose the second option, you are to blame. Nobody else but you. So, leave the living alone and go back to your hell hole for eternity'.*

You can forget reincarnation. Your soul is doomed to stay in that furnace they call hell. When you are causing havoc to the living, the head honchos that command you to cause havoc, terrify the people that you will never get a second chance at redemption. They know their goose is cooked.

That is why they continue to be nasty, they string you along to provoke fear in the minds of the human beings that are still enjoying life on this good old terra firma, so *'Get lost suckers!'*

One evening, I was sitting outside enjoying the nice temperature. For no apparent reason, I was punched in the stomach and thrown to the ground. I reached into my pocket, took out the mini bible and shoved it in the face of the malevolent spirit.

"Take this, fish face."

I felt a gust of wind and he was gone. A few months after receiving the comical blackmail letter, a lady who moved away from town gave me a call. I barely knew who she was. I remember, she used to reside right across the street from the supermarket.

She was upset at me because I did not find a way to contact her to advise her that her dad would die and for her to start making arrangements for her father to rest in peace.

She was livid; I could not interject. She would not shut her trap. I was thinking how can she breathe. Her lungs will run out of air; she will have to stop momentarily to catch her breath. She began verbally abusing me using foul language. I was finally able to say a few words.

"Do you kiss your mother with that dirty mouth?"

I ended the call. She called right back. She must have been using the speed dial on her phone. In a matter of seconds, she was again yelling and calling me names that I did not appreciate. I disconnected the call. She called a third time; I did not give her the time to start ranting and raving again.

"Listen, why don't you go take a happy pill. Go to the bathroom to take a crap so that it will take a load of your mind, shithead."

I hung up and left the phone of the hook. It's a shame calls like that one, will set me back on my heels. It takes the joy; the sense of accomplishment away replaced by anger and frustration. It's a good thing that I do not have to deal with those types of calls too often. I would have waved the white flag a long time ago. Well, life goes on. Tomorrow is another day.

I was visiting a friend; usually his dog greets me with his tail wagging. He is happy to see me. The dog will let me pet him. That day, he barked and looking behind me. I was pushed while removing my shoes. I came close to kissing the floor. Me, my friend, and his dog, were the only ones present in the house.

"Are you alright?"

"Yes, I am fine. I lost my balance."

"It's bizarre; that rover barked when you approached the door."

"He must have mistaken me for someone else."

The dog was now quiet. The entity was gone.

"You have been here more than once and he always greets you at the door; all happy to see you."

"No worries. No need to fuss over spilled milk. Dogs are like humans; like us they have good and bad days. Anyway, has the game started already?"

"No, but it is about to start. Want a beer?"

"You know that I do not drink anymore. Bring me a pop."

"Sorry, a force of habit."

"No sweat, I bet you my favorite player will get hat a trick tonight named: the first star of the game."

The dog was quiet and sleeping. I did not tell my friend why the dog was barking. The dog was able to see something following me. We were able to watch the game without having to deal with those pesky spirits. I was having a chat with Father Joseph. He inquired if my bad luck subsided.

"Yes, the bad luck has decreased."

"Do you want to know why? Your karmic debt has been paid."

"That is great news."

"Yes, it is great news; but do not forget the negative energy that you deal with will always bring you some bad luck."

"I did not know that my karmic debt was paid. Thank you for letting me know. I do not understand how you know the bad luck has decreased but I am still getting more than my fair share of bad luck."

"Yes, your personal karmic debt is paid that is why the bad luck has subsided a little bit. There is nothing you can do about the bad luck the entities bring."

"The last couple of times we talked, you did not mention anything about my debt being paid."

"At that time, your debt was not yet paid in full."

"Do you know if there is a way they could have eliminated my personal debt?"

"That would be nice, but no cigars. When was the last time you were over here giving me a headache?"

"I cannot recall. I know it's been awhile"

"At that time, there was still a small amount to be paid."

"How do you know that?"

"I go with what you reveal to me when you came over. I have your karmic chart in my office; every time we speak, I update your chart. That is why I inquired about your situation with your bad luck, your chart is now at zero. Congratulations."

"For real? My chart in your office?"

"Yes, that's right."

"Can I take a glimpse of that famous chart?"

"Come in my office; I will show you."

There it was: my own personal chart decorating the wall.

"One question, why have you not mentioned that you have my so called chart in your office?"

"The topic never came up. We were busy discussing events and your attitude towards things."

He took the time to educate me what certain symbols meant.

"I will be darned. Look at this beautiful painting on your wall; nice symbols. The question marks, scribbling and markings that I have no clue for what they stand for."

I was about to go home when he reminded me to be careful not to accumulate more karmic debt.

"If you notice that your bad luck is on the rise, that means you did something you knew was not the right thing to do and yet you did it anyway. Am I clear? Do you have a pretty good idea of what I just said?"

"I do; it's clear as mud. All kidding aside, I do understand."

On an accident scene, a teenage girl was screaming her lungs out due to the pain from her injuries. I did not know who she was, but she knew who I was. With tears in her eyes, she wanted me to save her.

"I know you talk to god. Tell him to save me please."

Although I could not do anything more for her; when the ambulance arrived, I reassured her.

"I will do my best to convince him to help you."

"Thank you so much. I hope that he does help me."

I knew she was not going to make it. She passed away on the operating table. To move on to the next 911 call you need to put these types of situations on the back burner-- it is never easy. To help me cope, I try to go to church every Sunday. One Sunday morning, a woman came up to me; another unknown.

"Can you please ask god to take me, instead of my son who is terminally ill? Why him? Why not take me? We are in the house of god; I beg you to talk to him."

I painfully had to tell her,

"I cannot change the outcome. I will pray for you. You should also pray to god and ask him the same question."

The conversation broke my heart. We do not get training to be able to handle different scenarios. The trainer would always say, 'when the going gets tough, the tough gets going'. Yes, you can say that when you are combatting a very large and difficult fire; not when it comes to human beings.

I wish the population would listen when I talk. They would be aware that I do not have the power to cure sick people, or perform miracles. When talking to her, I knew that her son only had a few months to live. I have not seen her since that Sunday morning. Who she was, where she came from, where she got her information to come and talk to me; I guess I will never know.

We as first responders, we witness graphic scenes that are hard to put into words; so much sadness. We were responding to a medical call. I remained outside to prevent people rushing into the house and interfere with our work. I was listening to the small talk from the onlookers across the street. I overheard one guy tell the others.

"He is the guy that can predict things. He will be able to let us know if the guy who lives there is in critical condition: if he is going to make it or not. Let's go and ask him."

Another bystander disagreed.

"Leave him alone. Let him do his job. These guys are sworn to secrecy. It is part of their code of conduct."

"I am crossing the street; I am going to ask him anyway. It is our right to know."

I turned around to ignore him. He was relentless wanting information. I lost it with this guy. A fellow firefighter had to intervene. The cops arrived ahead of the ambulance. They took over crowd control. Funny with the cops present at the scene, the onlookers were now nice and quiet; including the bimbo that was pushing all the wrong buttons.

It is a shame in situations like that one, that we cannot make a citizen arrest and be able to say like the series Miami Vice, book him Danno. After that incident, I took a leave of absence. It was getting to the point that I would smack a pest like that foolish rubbernecker and get into a whole lot of trouble.

I was like a pressure valve. I needed to release some steam. I booked an appointment to talk to my therapist after six months on sick leave; I rejoined my partners in crime. I make sure to book an appointment once a month to talk to my shrink, which helps me to cope with everyday life.

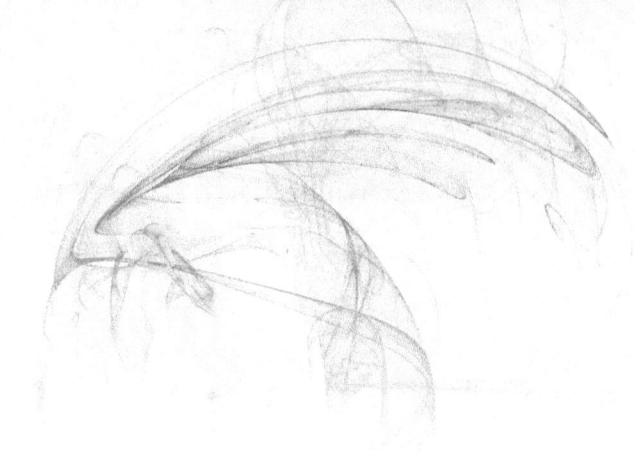

Chapter 16

One night, the devil decided to drop in for a visit. I could hear a low gruffy menacing voice that was coming from each corner of the house.

"I am the ultimate power. I will destroy you."

I responded.

"If I was you, I would not be so confident that you can destroy me. I have powerful allies."

"We will see. I will be back."

A few days later, it was the firefighter annual Christmas party. In the evening, pictures were taken and everybody was having a grand old time.

One of my partners in crime showed me the pictures that were taken a little earlier in the evening. In the background, you could see the devil and demons by his side. One of the entities must be the ringleader— red color, big horns and yellow eyes. I can tell you one thing: these entities were not camera shy. I said to my wife.

"Look, one of the female entities is applying a final touch of her makeup."

"Very funny! So you are a comedian tonight."

In the book, I have touched the subject of photos with spirits and demons. The photos disappear without a trace and were never seen again. Apparently, the photos are not to be seen by anyone. The photos were still in the digital camera when they vanished. The other photos in the camera are okay. Critics say they were deleted by error. Maybe once, but not every time the photos are taken.

Not a word was said about the photoshoot with the demons; everybody was having a blast. We did not want to disrupt the flow of the party. One night a year where we can gather to let loose and go crazy. We are all off duty. The neighboring fire department is always our backup for the evening and when it is time for their party, we return the favor.

I learned something from the party: that you can have fun without a drop of alcohol. We came home close to 3 A.M. We immediately hit the sack.

Right on cue exactly 3 A.M, bizarre low music came on. Sounds like some poor individual was in the process of being tortured. There was also some sobbing; the bedroom reeked of urine and rotting flesh. At 4 A.M, the entertainment was over.

No standing ovation for these outdated performers; we finally dozed off. The next morning, the floors were covered with dark stains. When I looked a little closer, the stains were dry blood. The significance of the blood stains was probably a preview of what might happen if I continue butting heads with them . The dogs did not bark; the reason why… I do not know.

It took all morning to clean the mess. We spent the remaining of the day cleansing the house. We rubbed holy water on the door frames. We placed a blessed crucifix in every room of the house in doorways, around our bed. The blessed bible that the priest gave me never left my side. I called Father Joseph to give him a report of what went down when we came home from the party.

"That is not a good sign. Dry blood stains on the floor. They have elevated their threat to another level. That means they will show no mercy; this is a matter of grave importance. I will contact the bishop and see what can be done. I will get back to you ASAP."

After the phone call, I explained to my wife all that was said between me and Father Joseph. I was nervous, concerned about our safety. I suggested to my wife that she should go spend time with her aunt until we can find a solution.

"No way, I will not leave you alone. I am staying right here with you. No ifs or buts about it. I am staying. I am not going to run and hide when you need me the most."

She gave me a big hug.

"We will fight together and show them what we are made of. If they think they can do whatever they want, they have another thing coming."

The same night that we cleansed the house, I wanted to stay awake as long as I could. Fatigue got the best of me. I fell asleep around two a.m. The night was peaceful. The following morning, Father Joseph called.

"The only thing we can do is resist; not give them an inch while they try to go forward. We will have to meet them head on; power against power and show no fear."

"You know that I always show no fear. I am not scared of anything."

"Yes I know but you never know. They will determine that fear is your weakness; they will try to capitalize on your fear. The bishop is packing his suitcase as we speak and will join us to do this battle. I will talk to you soon."

No disturbances for about a week. I kept Father Joseph updated. I would call him every morning. We were both under the assumption that my ritual was keeping us out of arms way; but that was not the case. The royal rumble began.

My wife was pushed out of bed by an unseen force. I woke up with fresh scratches on my arms, legs and stomach. The devil was inches from my face, squeezing the air out of me.

I was not able to breathe. The devil was on my stomach. He made sure that I was unable to move a finger. As I grew weaker, he was getting stronger-- draining my energy. I passed out. My wife said that the only way he released his grip is, she kept throwing holy water on him while reading from the bible.

When I regained consciousness, my wife was by my side washing my face with a cold wet towel. I had a hard time catching my breath; my neck was sore and bruised. My wife called Father Joseph. He made tracks, to come to bless the house and get rid of the vermins which I do not stand a chance of succeeding; to chase them away for good. Father Joseph was accompanied by a powerful man-- the archbishop.

"It's time to take out the big guns."

When they were done blessing the house, they warned me. They will come back tonight. The blessing of the house became a sleepover for the priest and the bishop. Man! I was nervous and on edge. The wait was killing me. As predicted by the bishop, they came back.

This time, I was ready with the big artillery. The devil came face to face with Father Joseph. Father Joseph was reciting a ritual from a very old book. The bishop stood his ground. He was spreading holy water and salt everywhere.

They were both shoved a few times; but they were relentlessly reading from the book. The bishop is yelling at the devil and his friends, while he was still spraying the room with holy water. He looked at me.

"Burn some sage, lots of it."

I did what he requested. The bishop was now on his knees; he grabbed a big crucifix from his bag. The fight lasted for about an hour. The devil and his companions retreated. Before leaving, they all screamed at the same time. I will never forget that scream as long as I live. The bishop took a big breath.

"What a relief! They are gone. He is very powerful and I do not think that he has said his last words. He will comeback one way or another.

The priest and the bishop were both exhausted.

"I was so nervous wondering what might happen, especially to my wife."

"We will take a power nap and bless the house one more time."

"A big thank you to both of you."

In the morning, they blessed the house one more time. The bishop had this to say.

"What an incredible fight last night… but we prevailed. When Father Joseph told me you needed help, that was an understatement to say the least. Here is a prayer that you can recite every night before going to bed. Recite the prayer nine times and kiss the crucifix. Hopefully it will keep them away."

Before leaving, Father Joseph had this to say.

"The blood stains on the floor was an indication that you were doomed. Boy, did we turn the table on him. So long until the next adventure."

Every night, I recite the prayer and kiss the crucifix. So far so good, no more manifesting of spirits. I can now enjoy a good night sleep. I do not feel sluggish in the morning anymore. I hope the trend continues. People keep knocking on my door in search of answers. One day, a woman with cancer came knocking on my door. She was unknown to me; I had never seen her before.

"I have cancer. Is there a way that you can please see what the future holds for me? I have prepared myself for the worse; I did not want to make a fool of myself, if the answer to the question is negative."

I was curious to know who she was, where she came from, and how did she get my name and address. She introduced herself. She was polite. I could tell that she was a no nonsense woman. She lived an hour away; one of her friends who lives in town gave her the details on how to find me.

"I hope I am not interrupting. Silly me, I should have called before coming over. If it is too much of an inconvenience today, can I come back?"

"No, no, that's fine. You are not interrupting anything. Did your friend mentioned that I am not a medium and I cannot perform miracles?"

"Yes, she did. All I want to know if I have a fighting chance to beat this dreaded disease."

"OK, if you don't mind, I need to close my eyes and put my hand on your shoulder; is it okay with you?"

"Of course, go ahead. Do what you have to do."

I closed my eyes and I put my hand on her shoulder. It was summertime, I could see grass, snow, grass, snow, grass again, and so on. I was also getting positive vibes going in her direction. Before giving her an answer, I advised her.

"What I am about to tell you, I tell everybody the same thing. The situation may change, I have no control over that."

"No worries, I understand."

"You have people praying for you, am I right? Because I could feel positive vibes going in your direction."

"Yes, my friends and family."

"Well, you can tell your friends and family that their prayers will be answered. Remember if things change, please do not come back to beat me or give me a hard time."

"Silly you, of course not!"

"Over the years, it has occurred a few times that my prediction changed. Like I said, I have no control over the changes."

"No worries, I am a calm person and I truly appreciate what you are doing for me today."

"Good news, you will be victorious with your war against cancer. The way I can tell it is when I put my hand on your shoulder and close my eyes. If it is summertime, I will see grass, then snow, grass, snow and so on.

"I hope you have seen a lot of grass and snow and so on for me."

"In your case, I was able to see grass, snow and so on. I could not see a dead end. Do not get me wrong, you have a big hill to climb but you will make it to the top and also, keep in mind that things may change."

"I completely understand. Thank you so much."

She was crying.

"The tears are tears of joy."

She reached for her wallet.

"Put that away. I will never accept money for what I do. You guys have enough to worry about, without having to worry about financial problems. Can I ask you one favor?"

"Of course."

"Please try not to give my name to your acquaintances."

"You have my word."

About a year later, I heard a knock at the door. When I opened the door, there she was. She gave me a big hug.

"I am now cancer-free. What you told me that day really helped me to keep going. I did not want to be a statistic in your small majority of a different outcome for your visions."

"I completely understand."

"I did not divulge your name. It is still a secret."

"Thank you. I really respect the fact that you kept your word and you have not given my name to anyone."

"I am a person that keeps her word. Well, goodbye."

And she was on her way. The visit for me was incredible for my morale; it did wonders for my mojo. The fact that she drove one hour instead of giving me a call to thank me; and the best of all, she kept my name a secret. She is one in a million. I am very happy for her.

A few weeks later, someone came knocking at my door. To my surprise, I was looking at an identical twins.

"We are identical twins."

"Yes, I can see that."

She let me know they were twenty-six years old.

"The reason for our visit is, my sister is very sick."

"Did she go see a doctor?"

"No. With all the information we could dig up on you, we were under the assumption that you would be able to help us. Am I right by believing that you cure sick people? My sister has been coughing up blood for a week now. "

"Please go see a doctor."

"We are identical twins, sometimes we can feel each other's anguish.

I reiterated my words,

"Please go see a doctor. I am sure she will be alright."

"How can you tell me that she will be fine?"

"I already told you. I do not heal sick people; I can only see things."

"I am afraid that if she dies, I might also die. Can we get it in writing that you mentioned she will get better?"

"Goodnight."

As I was opening the door to go back in the house, she let me know that she was not pleased with me.

"You do not have to be such an ass."

"I am sorry if you feel that way. Again, goodnight and go back where you dug up the information on me and fill the hole."

"Silly! It was not a real hole. We did not dig a hole."

I shook my head and closed the door,

"Where do they come from? A funny farm?"

Walking to their car, I could see they were talking; hands in the air, and they finally drove away. I cannot comprehend the fact that they came to see me, thinking I could cure her. The information, like she said, dug up on me and not only that, the sick twin did not utter a word. My wife joined me in the kitchen.

"What was that all about?"

"They came here thinking I cure sick people. Whoever gave them the information that I can cure sick people was dead wrong; no pun intended. I can say that they are both out of their minds thinking I would be able to perform a miracle to cure her sister instead of seeing a doctor."

"You should know by now; things will never change."

"I wish them luck. What a relief they are gone. It is this kind of confrontation that really puts my patience to the test. My opinion is, they are a few bricks short of a load."

"Now, now, honey."

"Well, it's true."

I cannot go anywhere without an individual seeking details or information from me. I was at the post office, a woman hurried to cross the street to get to me. I was in my truck leaving the parking lot.

"I nearly missed you, are you the guy that knows what will happen in the future? As you can see, I am pregnant, and I am in my fourth month. I want to know if my baby will be healthy for many years to come?"

"Can I put my hand on your shoulder?"

"Why do you need to put your hand on my shoulder? Is this a trick to fool me or something?"

"I can assure you it is no trick."

"OK, OK, go ahead."

"All I can tell you is, there will be no complications giving birth. As for the health of your newborn, the doctor will be able to tell you."

"The doctor is not a psychic; you are."

I jumped back in my truck and drove away before she said another word. A couple of days later, an expecting mother knocked at my door. She quoted,

"I am having a terrible pregnancy."

She was worried. Her sister had numerous complications giving birth to her first baby. Her other sister had to deal with the agony of losing her baby in the final weeks of pregnancy.

"It was catastrophic for her. It was the end of the world for her when she lost her baby. She went into shock and was in denial for over a month. That was eleven months ago and she still feels the pain of losing her baby. What you will tell me today, I might consider an abortion."

I put my hand on her shoulder. I advised her not to be worried.

"Yes, you will continue having some difficulties; but you will be able to see the light at the end of the tunnel when you reach the light. You will give birth to a healthy baby."

"What a relief! This is a big weight off my shoulders. I was hoping to hear some marvelous words."

She acknowledged that she understood things may change.

"Going forward. I now have a lot of confidence."

Mom and the baby are doing fine. A little boy was sitting on the side of a sidewalk sobbing; his dog was hit by a car. The dog suffered only minor injuries. I told the young man,

"Ask your mom or dad to bring your dog to a vet. He will recuperate from his wounds."

As I was leaving, the boy's parents arrived. The boy's parent brought the dog to the vet and the dog recuperated from his wounds. I always rejoice when I can spot white shadows or angels from a short distance. It elevates my confidence, especially when I am struggling with difficult manifestations.

I put my trust in their help. In a lot of events, I would not be able to overcome some obstacles in order to complete the task at hand without their help. Wherever I am, my days are hampered by events. Death does not wait for anyone. Death is an enemy we cannot defeat. I could be taking a walk on a nice sunny day, playing sports. It does not matter where I am. Spirits find me.

I need time to find a spot so that I can be alone. These situations have caused a lot of irritation, impatience, and a few choices of words with teammates, also with some spectators. Some disgruntled fans say it is a ruse that I concocted, so that my team can to be able to end up in the win column.

I am the goaltender in hockey, and a pitcher when playing ball. The game cannot proceed until I resurface to finish the match. There is no time frame for events: some wake me up in the middle of the night. No nine-to-five job for me.

Thank god, these scenarios are far in between. At a fundraiser, I was in the middle of a speech when suddenly a spirit needed help to get to heaven. I told the audience that I received an urgent message on my phone; I would be back in fifteen minutes. A spirit needing guidance interrupted one of my monthly sessions with my therapist. She was looking over my shoulder pointing in my direction.

"What is that?"

I turned around to take a look. I saw a white light.

"Do not to be alarmed, this is perfectly normal."

"Maybe for you but not for me."

As usual I went into my own little world, when it was over. I noticed my therapist was looking at me with disbelief in her eyes.

"Where did you go? You were like a statue for about fifteen minutes?"

In the middle of my trance she noticed a few black shadows.

"When we talked about the topic about your ability to guide souls to heaven, I gave you the benefit of the doubt. Now that I witnessed it with my own eyes, I am now on board as your ship captain."

I took the time to explain the significance of the light, the trance and the black shadows.

"I am somewhat offended that you had doubts that I was not telling you the truth. I do not come here to make up ludicrous make-believe fantasy stories to embellish myself and certainly not to insult your intelligence."

"I am sorry, some clients come in with the intention of stuffing me like a turkey with false statements. They are afraid to tell the truth as to why they come to see me and lie is beyond me. I will never again doubt anything you say."

"I can appreciate that, but you cannot put all the apples in the same basket."

"That was supposed to be the topic for our next session. I was going to tell you that I was giving you the benefit of the doubt and see if you were going to change your story. Believe me when I say it was not personal, like I said, a great majority of clients do lie."

"I have no doubt that some do lie but you should be able to know with different questions pertaining to the same topic."

"Yes, I know. It is a strategy that I use; my indication that the client is truthful or full of baloney."

"You said you were going to test me in our next session."

"Yes I was, but we will discuss another topic next month. You know that our conversations are always confidential. What is said in this room stays in this room."

"Yes, I am aware of that."

"Anyway, if I was to tell someone what I witnessed today; they would probably think or mention that I am the one that needs therapy. Boy, what you do is incredible."

I thanked her for her time. Before leaving, I noticed a frown in her face.

"Are you alright? You look as if you are in a daze or something."

"I am fine. It's just hard to comprehend what I just witnessed. I am bewildered that an individual can do what you do. I will see you in a month."

A group of hometown folks came knocking at my door. They wanted me to teach them what to do, in order for them to make money.

"You guys have the audacity to come to my home for such purposes of making money with a ludicrous request? This is hilarious! You guys were joking right?"

"We are not amused but insulted at your response."

"Go home, please. Leave me alone."

"You do not want to teach us because you want to be the only one making all the money."

"Goodbye, dimwits."

I closed the door.

"I need to do something about all this nonsense or else, I will spend the rest of my days wearing a straitjacket."

I came up with the idea to rent the town hall. I invited every citizen from town, including neighboring towns. I had posters made that everyone was welcomed. People came in droves which was great because it cost me a pretty penny to rent the hall.

I littered the town and our neighboring towns with posters. If someone tells me he did not see any posters he or she must be blind. Hopefully this idea will educate the population about the things I can do and cannot do.

I prepared a ton of material to talk about. I was hoping when people would leave, they will know the color of my underwear. I wanted to be as thorough as possible even with the smallest of details. When everyone was seated. I introduced myself. Some lame brain shouted.

"We all know who you are."

"The reason for this gathering here tonight is to try to make you understand that I am an ordinary citizen like everyone else."

A shout from the crowd.

"You are not like us; you can do magic."

"Like I was saying, I have a sixth sense."

People were still chatting among themselves. I yelled out.

"Can everyone pay attention and listen to what I have to say?"

A man from the crowd shouted.

"Could everyone kindly shut up? I want to hear what he has to say. I cannot understand you people, you come here for information and you are not listening. You're wasting your time, my time and his time."

"Thank you, sir."

"No sweat."

Still a lot of chatter until I blurted out one thing.

"I forgot to mention that there is a twenty-dollar fee to attend. There will be a collection plate at the door when you leave."

The hall was quiet. You could hear the crickets outside.

"As soon as I said, 'a fee from everyone', all of you paid attention. There is no fee. It was a ploy to get everyone's attention. Now I need a moment of your time. So please pay attention to what I am about to say."

I was interrupted by someone in the crowd.

"Is it going to be long, to say what you have to say? I do not have all night, you know."

"Just listen please, and we will be out of here in no time. That way, there will be no excuses to come irritate me and say I did not know. I am not a saint. I cannot walk on water. I cannot perform miracles and most of all, magically cure the sick or disabled individuals."

I spent over an hour talking, explaining in simple words that everybody would understand. I hope that I was clear enough in French and English. As usual, some were not listening. A lady in the front row did not stop flapping her gums. I would guess, about sixty percent understood what I said; the other forty percent did not listen.

"I interrupted Miss chatterbox by asking her.

"Does it make sense what I wanted the population to know?"

"hummm."

"Of course not."

I pointed a finger at some individuals.

"You, you and you, same thing. You have no clue what I was talking about. It is a shame; we are all supposed to be adults, but I couldn't help but notice a lot of you are still in infancy, cannot stay quiet and listen for a few minutes."

It's like talking to a hall filled with five-year-olds. The ones that did not listen drilled me with so many questions, with no time in between questions to at least answer one question. One particular question was,

"When will the lunch be served? We are starving."

The attendees were talking among themselves. I exited the hall and drove home. No one even noticed that I left the premises. Hopefully the ones that understood my message will educate the others who did not understand; and the ones that did not take the time to listen to a word I said. What a waste of money and time!

Several days later, I was approached by a woman. She wanted to let me know that I was a human angel. I wondered if she attended last week's meeting. So anyway, she also mentioned helping so many fellowmen, when they need a hand. All the volunteer work that I do. She was one of the directors for the united way which is a great organization, who helps those in need.

"Believe me, I am no angel. I have faults like everybody else-- bad habits, guilty numerous sins. Thank you. I know you mean well with your kind words. I do what I can to help. If I am an angel, well every volunteer on the planet are also angels."

"If you put that way, you are right; we are all angels."

"I never considered myself an angel and never will. I see myself as a good person with a good heart. Some human beings did or are still doing today a lot more than me. They are not recognized as angels, it's a darn shame. Did you come all the way over here to tell me that I am an angel?"

"Yes and no, I was wondering if you wanted to be one of our directors for the united way?"

"I am flattered but I am afraid the answer is no. I have enough on my plate as it is."

"Are you sure?"

"Yes."

"I understand."

She made her way back to her car. If I had a dollar every time I answered these questions: '*do you see angels on a daily basis?*',or '*Do they all look the same and why themselves are unable to see the angels?*' I would have a six digit bank account.

I see the heavenly beings or angels when I need their help. Angels are not always the way we see them in books, or in paintings. They can be in the form of white shadows: some have wings, some are human angels that walk among us.

If you are in a crisis and you ask god for help, he will send angels to help you. They may choose to be seen, or some not wanting to be seen; depends on the crisis that you need their assistance. If you see a glowing light, wings, a white mist, or a white shadow, you are not hallucinating.

They are angels that have answered your call for help. Some angels can be strangers offering their help. When they are no longer needed, they will walk away. You will probably never see them again. They are among us, and they come from all walks of life.

I was at a bar with friends, enjoying nonalcoholic drinks. I had a hunch, that the couple sitting a few tables from us, the man was about to strike his wife in the face. I told my friends about my hunch.

"Come on, now. You mean to tell me."

He did not have time to finish his sentence. The man gets up from his chair punches his wife in the face. He was about to deliver a second blow when one of the bouncers at the bar escorted the man to the door. The poor lady was crying. She made her way to the bar to get some ice to put on her cheek.

I took the opportunity to warn her that I have a bad feeling if she went home. Some harm might come to her.

"I have nowhere else to go; besides he is my husband. I love him. He must be feeling some remorse for striking me. I am sure when I get home, he will apologize."

So, she went home. She was badly beaten by her husband. Needing hospitalization, her husband is in jail. When I got word of what happened, I told my friend,

"Remember the couple who was arguing in the bar last night?"

"Yes."

"Guess what, she is now in the hospital after a severe beating from her husband. Her coward husband is in jail."

"It is still beyond me how you can do that. I am sure when you got out of bed yesterday, that you were aware some lady would be punched in the face by her husband."

"Of course not, you know that I am not a medium. If I am in the vicinity where something is about to happen, I get a hunch a feeling that something out of the ordinary is about to unfold."

My friend shook his head.

"I will always be in the fog, trying to make sense on how you proceed to know these things."

"You have to live it to understand."

I was at a water park with my daughter. It was a very hot scorching day. My daughter wanted to go home.

"Dad, it's way too hot today. I want to go home."

"We will go home in a few minutes."

Someone started yelling for help. I ran to see if I could be of assistance. A young black teenager was woozy, incoherent and she fainted. I provided first aid assistance until the paramedics arrived. I provided the paramedics with the pertinent information they needed to know. With my information and the paramedics' observations, we concluded that she was suffering from heat stroke.

A bystander blurted out.

"She cannot be suffering from a heatstroke."

"What observation from your part that made you come up with the conclusion that she is not suffering from a heat stroke? Did I miss something? I don't think so."

"She is black. Black people cannot get sunburns or sunstrokes because of their skin color."

"You moron."

"Well, it is true."

One of the paramedics was looking at me and at the new field doctor.

"Sir, we really appreciate your diagnosis. It's always a good thing when there is a doctor on site to lend a hand. Would you mind getting in the ambulance to watch over the patient until we reach the hospital or provide us with your phone number in case we need you in an emergency?"

The paramedic jumped into the ambulance.

"Sir, are you coming with us or what?"

The paramedic was looking at me with a big grin on his face, closed the ambulance doors and they were on their way to the hospital. I looked at him.

"So do you think she will make it to the hospital?"

"Shut up."

Some bystanders were mocking him by asking him questions about health issues. He looked at me and if eyes could kill, I would not be writing this book. I looked at him and walked to my car. I told my daughter.

"Remember the advice that I am going to give you. When you hear stupid comments like that one, do not waste your time looking for answers because there are none."

"I will make sure to remember, dad. Now I know why you wanted to stay a little while longer. You had one of your hunches, right dad?"

"Yes, that was the reason I wanted to stay a little while longer. Let's go home."

"Dad, can we stop for ice cream on the way home?"

"Yes, I guess we can do that."

Chapter 17

One night while asleep, I wandered out of the house and woke up in a snowbank-- shivering and cold. The back door was wide open. I took a couple of glances to my right, then to my left. Everything was quiet. I scooted back in the house. I was freezing.

I was puzzled as to why I was sleepwalking. Why would I go outside in the freezing cold? My wife was still asleep. I climbed back into my warm bed. I was not able to go back to sleep. My brain was racing a mile a minute trying to decipher a reason as to why I would venture outside in the cold.

Again, I went seeking knowledge from my dear trusted friend Father Joseph. He inquired if it was the first time for me to be sleepwalking?

"Besides from being drunk and falling asleep outside yes. It's been a few days now, everything seems to be back to normal. In the morning, I wake up in my bed with no signs of sleepwalking during the night."

"Alrighty then. We can rule out sleepwalking because if you start to walk in your sleep, it becomes a ritual. You walk in your sleep almost every night."

"Maybe, it was only a one-time thing."

"Maybe, but there must be a reason. Do you remember anything from that night?"

"Come to think of it. I can actually recollect. I remember, I was in a strange environment-- a place I have never seen before. It was all empty space. Absolutely nothing as far as the naked eye could see. I vaguely recall a dark blue color. That's all I can remember; except waking up in a bed made of snow."

"What you just described to me, I am quite positive that you were travelling from one newly discovered dimension to another. Something interrupted you to throw you off your path. You were looking for a way home; maybe that's why you ended up outside in the cold. Can you remember why you were distracted?"

"No."

"Think hard. If you have a smidgen of an image, tucked away in your head."

"Noooo… yes, wait a minute. There was a strange light coming towards me and I woke up in the snowbank."

"Did you observe if there was something in the light or around it? Was it a white light?"

"Yes, a white light. It was a little bigger and not quite the same shape that I usually see. Maybe there was a collision."

"I do not recall hearing of collisions travelling from one dimension to another. As a matter of fact, it is not supposed to happen. I will do some research."

A few weeks later, Father Joseph gave me a call to tell me that he came up empty. He could not find any information as to why I woke up in a snowbank.

"Thanks, I really appreciate that you took the time to do some research for me."

"You're welcome. Until next time."

"You bet and rest assured there will be many next times. A lot of strange things going on in both worlds that we cannot explain."

"That is an understatement to say the least, my friend."

"So long, my friend."

"So long and try to stay safe."

"I will try but no guaranties."

With today`s technology improving like the speed of light, the critics now have all the ammunition they need to analyze events. Scientists say they know the secrets of miracles. They can debunk the paranormal.

I do know for a fact that they are wasting valuable time and money trying to prove that spirits, ghosts do not exist. They should use the time and money to find a cure for some devastating diseases.

But no, they need to prove us wrong. Well, good luck with new technology; machines made by humans, software made by humans. There is no way a machine can prove that there is no such thing as miracles, the paranormal and demons. The devices cannot see or feel what humans can feel. Machines are always waiting for a command from a human to know what to do. I rest my case.

I was in bed tossing and turning unable to sleep. My wife was by my side.

"You are not able to sleep because of too much baggage that you keep in that brain of yours."

"No, it`s a case of insomnia."

"Keep convincing yourself it's insomnia. What you need to do is getting rid of everybody else`s luggage. It's time for a good cleanup or else your head will explode. It's easy to clean: you take a rag, insert the rag in the left or right ear and grab the rag when it comes out the opposite side."

"Very funny. It`s as funny as a bus full of pregnant nuns."

"Do what you have to do; stop feeling guilty for no reason. If something goes wrong, it is not your fault. You did the best you could. You know as well as I do that things do not always go according to plan. Close your eyes and start cleaning."

"OK, it might take a while."

"Take all the time you need."

"Easier said than done."

"You need to make sure your burden of guilt goes away for good. It does not have to be done in one day. A little bit every day, trust me you will feel as if a load of bricks was removed from your shoulders. "

"I will let you know when I am done cleaning my brain."

We decided to take a vacation. A change of scenery would be good for the both of us. I booked a room at a very nice establishment located on an island resort. The view from our room was spectacular. We could see the ocean, palm trees, and the beach. So, we settled in for the week.

We were relaxing, enjoying the sun while at the beach; having a few drinks at the bar and pop for me, taking moonlight strolls on the beach, making new friends, everything was great. Until one night, one of the guest at the hotel was heading to his room which is two doors down the hall from our room.

Apparently, he observed a black shadow go through our door. Once in his room, he called security to let them know that something strange was manifesting in our room; maybe some black magic. We were both in bed when we heard a knock on the door. I got up and answered the door. Two men from the hotel security were standing at the door.

"A guest called security to complain that he witnessed a black shadow entering your room. He is terrified of ghosts and is afraid that you are maybe practicing black magic, and you are maybe putting a curse on the resort."

"That is nonsense. We were both in bed asleep."

"Nonetheless sir, can we come in and take a look?"

"Sure, go ahead. Knock yourselves out. You will not find any magic potions, strange ritual books a black pot and so on."

"I am sorry sir, but we need to follow the hotel`s protocol and do a search of the room."

"Do what you have to do."

They searched our room and did not find anything out of the ordinary.

"Well, what is the verdict: guilty or not guilty?"

"Not guilty."

"Like I told you, we were both in bed."

"We apologize for the inconvenience, sir."

"It`s OK. You guys need to do your jobs. I applaud you for a job well done. I feel a lot safer now knowing you guys are on the job. I must admit, I was nervous that I might end up in the slammer. May I inquire who made the complaint?"

"We are not at liberty to say, sir."

"It does not matter. I know it`s the weirdo, two doors down."

"Why do you say he is a weirdo?"

"Follow him for a few hours, you will get your answer. Go tell him the good news: no demons and goblins in our room. I am sure, he will be happy with the news. Well, goodnight."

I closed the door.

"There was no need to be sarcastic you smartass."

"Well, I`d rather be a smartass than a dumbass. We cannot go on vacation without being harassed. So much for a peaceful vacation, everything was going great until tonight, there is no escape."

"Yes, I know. But it's OK."

"I can understand a spirit coming to see me. I knew it might happen, but this far-fetched assumption is ludicrous, black magic, really. I have a notion to go knock on his door; and when he opens the door. I punch his big honking schnozzle."

"I was not asleep. I could feel a presence in the room. The knocking on the door scared away whatever was in the room."

"Really? I am the man of the house. I wonder why I did not notice a presence in the room?"

"It's hard to be the man of the house when you're snoring."

Fortunately for us, it was the only incident. We were able to enjoy the remaining of our vacation without another glitch, which was great.

I get a lot of inquiries from the public if I see god. I keep advising those who keep pestering me on knowing. *'If you are that curious to know, go to church read the bible then you will know that god is with us every day'*; but they want to know if I physically see god in any shape or form?

The answer is NO. God does not venture much. He remains in his office and let his employees tackle the tasks at hand, but rest assured he is always keeping an eye on us from a distance. I sure would love to make his acquaintance shake his hand, feel his power, knowledge, and his true kindness. For me, it would be a dream come true.

Another inquiry that comes my way quite often: If I get the same feeling… if it is someone in the family that needs assistance, for example, your uncle, cousins? Yes and no when I am aware that one of my siblings will kick the bucket. I can block the sentiments that I feel. Otherwise, I would not be able to control my emotions.

My family is aware that I can block some of my feelings when it comes to them. If I would not be able to do so, they would be able to see the agony in my face. They would get suspicious that I am hiding something.

Do not get me wrong, I know their time is coming but I do not know when. The whole family would want to know when their time will come, which I do not blame them for wanting to know. By blocking the premonition, I am unable to provide any information to anyone.

Nobody wants to know any morbid details and circle a date on the calendar with an estimated day he or she has left to be among the living and be with their family and friends. The feeling is certainly not the same when it implicates someone close to you.

The holiday is a festive season; when families get together, party with friends filled with joy, and make memories that will last a lifetime. I feel for the family who lost a loved one during the holiday season and needs guidance. It makes a huge dent in the holiday festivities that I enjoy so much.

During the holidays when a spirit comes to me for guidance, I have to admit that it is extremely hard to concentrate and focus on what needs to be done. The devil does not give a damn about the holidays. He never stops searching for souls to bring back with him in his hell hole. Like I previously mentioned, death does not wait for anyone.

A little note on why it is important for the souls not to be intimidated to turn left when they should be turning right on the highway to heaven. That is why guidance is so important; anyway, here is a note that will explain what I am talking about.

(*The devil tries to throw you off your path; you have a path to god. It`s that road less traveled that regardless of what life presents, leads to god. The devil tries his best to throw you off that path. He whispers in your ear anything that will make you doubt your direction in life...there you go folks. This is a known fact.*)

When your time has come to leave this world, it is your last curtain call on this earth. The lights went out for one last time. One Christmas Eve, we laid my little cousin to rest. It was painful, I was one of two pallbearers. A small casket… what a shame poor little dude to be put in the ground on Christmas Eve. He was only three years old.

Another Christmas Eve, another one of my cousins passed away. She came home from work. She collapsed while cooking dinner; a massive heart attack. She was dead before hitting the floor. The mom of one of my close friends passed away on Christmas morning.

It is heart-wrenching. Like I previously said, the season that we should be enjoying, celebrating the new year instead, are filled with agony and pain. Every Christmas is a constant reminder of their loved ones who are gone, like they say, to a better place. There is a saying that, *Time heals everything*. I am still waiting for some personal events to heal.

Time does not heal everything. It helps you cope so that you can move on. The sad part is, we all know it could happen to each and every one of us to lose someone dear to us over the holidays.

For me, some holiday seasons are more pleasant than other holiday seasons. I did not have the burden of guiding a soul into heaven. The worst holiday season for me so far was when three individuals passed away. I did what I had to do. These events are embedded in my brain. A month before Christmas, a ten year old little girl came knocking at my door.

"My mommy wants to know if you can delay my daddy from dying until after Christmas so that we can have a final Christmas with him."

The little girl was holding back her tears.

It's okay to cry when you are sad."

"My mom told me not to cry when talking to you."

"Why?"

"My mom said that it would look too obvious."

"Obvious for what? How come your mommy did not come herself to talk to me?"

"My mommy said if it was me talking to you instead of her, you would say yes. My dad is in the hospital and cannot come home for Christmas. He is always sleeping when we visit. The doctor said, my dad can still hear us talking. I keep asking him to wake up. The doctor also told my mom that it is only a matter of time before he dies."

"I am truly sorry. You do not know how sorry and painful sweetheart this is, a request that I am unable to deliver. All I can say, I will pray for your dad. Your family should also pray and ask god to delay the passing of your dad."

"My mommy told me you could."

"Where is your mom?"

"She is in the car waiting for me."

"I will go talk to your mom."

I made my way toward the car, and motioned for her mom to step out of the car.

"My little girl is crying, what did you tell her? My husband is a recipient of a heart transplant. Even with a ton of pills, his system keeps rejecting the new heart. There is nothing else they can do for him."

"Believe me when I say that I feel for your family, but why did you send your little girl for such a request? I do not know where you get your information. I cannot perform miracles. You should be ashamed for sending your little girl to see me, giving her false hope."

"I told her not to cry, it would be too obvious."

"Obvious for what? That part I do not understand. Do you realize for her now that it is a double whammy for her? Do you think it was easy for me when I told her that I could not help her from preventing her dad from dying before Christmas?"

"But I thought you could help us."

"I won't comment on what you just said. I know that you are in a sad situation, and I can appreciate that, but sending her to talk to me… please leave before I say something that I might regret. So please go."

What am I supposed to say to my daughter?"

"It is up to you to think of something; not me. Please go."

As she was driving away, I shook my head in disbelief. Poor little girl, she will lose her dad and be stuck with a mom like that. This is one of the reasons why my patience is dwindling away. Another individual poking his nose where it does not belong. I call him the maintenance man who works for Father Joseph. He saw me leaving Father Joseph's office.

"You have again needed his help. What is the matter, you cannot find your own answers?"

I stopped walking. I gave him a dirty look and started walking in his direction.

"Do I really need to reply to the question? I do not think so. Let me ask you a question: what is it to you that I come to see him? Does it give you extra work like sweeping the floor when I leave or what?"

"No."

"Why the unnecessary comments?"

"You are right. I apologize, it is none of my business. I had nothing to gain with my remarks; it was nasty on my part."

"If it is going to make you sleep better at night knowing, I need to keep him in the loop on certain matters so when I need his assistance, he has a clear picture of what I am trying to tell him. Yes, I do have many questions; some he cannot answer. I have to be very diligent on some of the issues."

With a smile he said,

"The last time you were here, it crossed my mind that you two were indulging in passion, you know… love."

"You never know what goes on behind closed doors, you can always join us."

He stood there looking at me.

"Now that you know and you don't have anything to say. What about my invitation for you to join us?"

While shaking his head, he answered

"No. I now have an image in my head of you two enjoying the pleasures of the flesh."

"Do you want to spice up your image by joining us?"

"God, no!"

"Come on, it's only a joke. I had you wondering if all of this is true."

"Yes, you had me going for a minute. You're good. I guess you need to be on your toes to answer dumb questions like mine."

"You have no idea my friend. The nonsense, ridiculous comments that come my way are almost everyday. Over the years, I have mastered the skill of quickly putting a blanket on the pile of cheap shots from ignorant people.

"Yes, I now know to not ask you stupid questions."

"When I am done, they stand there with their mouths wide open with nothing to say; and swallowing insects like you are doing right now. Have a good evening talk to you later."

My wife is always worried that I might not be able to come back when I am in a trance, that is why she counts the minutes. She says that my average is between eight to twelve minutes. For her, it is like an eternity.

"When I am in a trance, do you see a light in front of me?"

"No, why?"

"I wanted to make sure because it is supposed to be only me that can have a visual of the light when I am guiding a soul. Also, when angels are helping me to guide the spirits upstairs to the big house."

"On occasions, I see you struggling."

"How can you tell?"

"By your movements and gestures, if everything is as it should be, you are like a statue."

"Yes, entities try to interfere and disrupt the process. It is not always smooth sailing. I am grateful that angels lend me a hand without their assistance. Some souls would be dragged to hell never to return. "

"I am a bit confused when you asked me if I could see the light when you're guiding a soul to heaven, but I often see the light coming towards you."

"Lights are visible when they are coming towards me; and when I start the process of guiding the souls, we go into a sort of funnel and sometimes the souls will make themselves invisible. I am the only one that can see them."

While having a chat with Father Joseph, he raised the subject of exorcism; if I would like to be present when one is performed? I declined the invitation for the simple reason: if I am in the room where the exorcism is taking place. The priest performing the exorcism may ask for my help. I want none of that. I have way too much on my plate as it is.

"I remember that we touched on the subject before. I wanted to know if you still feel the same way."

"As you can see, the feelings are still the same; so far so good. I have not yet met an individual who was possessed by a demon. I plan on keeping it that way."

It is no picnic when you deal with the public; do not get me wrong by saying these words. It is the pressure of what needs to be done. I cannot afford to miss a beat when dealing with the expectations of the people and their hope for good news.

Some cry, some cannot deal with the reality of losing a loved one. Some accept their fate and some simply do not believe a word I say. It seems nowadays in the news on television, the newspapers and social media, all we hear or read is about murders, suicide bombers, violence and wars.

But what I have seen over the years, there is still an abundance of love, generosity, good and kind people in the world that we live in. It seems that we always feed on the negativity, rarely on the positive side of things.

In emergencies, I have seen strangers helping strangers. Deep down, we need to believe that everyone has some goodness in their heart. When it is time to show the compassion that still exist in our troubled society, someone will always step up to the plate by helping their fellow man.

They roll up their sleeves, open their wallets, do what needs to be done. Too bad, it is overshadowed by all the negative publicity. The greedy ones take advantage of circumstances to inflate their bank accounts, no remorse no scruples whatsoever. I call that type of person an *icicle*-- born with a cold heart and they will die with a wallet full of money and a cold empty heart.

I was in bed reading a book, my wife was in the living room.

"Are you talking to me or your sister who passed away?"

"No, why? You know I am not a silent reader. I read as if I am talking to someone."

"I heard her voice calling your name."

I looked at the window and there she was. Her message was to be careful in the kitchen. I took the time to check everything the whole nine yards. I could not find anything that was defective that would be the cause for an alarm.

I checked the smoke detectors and fire extinguishers; like I said, the whole nine yards. My carbon monoxide detector was on its last legs. I took a ride to the hardware store and came home with a brand-new detector.

The kind you need to plug into an electrical outlet that also includes a battery in case of a power outage. My previous detector ran on batteries. I was looking for an outlet where I could plug in the new detector.

The phone rang, it was one of my buddies. We talked for about twenty minutes. When I was done talking to my friend on the phone and finding an outlet for carbon monoxide, the detector and batteries slipped my mind. I joined my wife in the living room to watch a movie.

That same night while sleeping, I was shoved hard enough to wake me up. I was very drowsy, and I could smell propane. I made my way to the kitchen, one of the burners on the stove was not properly turned off.

I opened a few windows. You have to be very careful when it comes to propane stoves. They can be a silent killer. The knob was between the on and off button just enough that we were not able to smell the propane before going to bed. I woke up my wife. I told her the reason I was waking her up in the middle of the night.

"The new detector you purchased must be defective; we did not have any warning."

It dawned on me the new carbon monoxide detector was not plugged into the outlet and without any batteries. Unbelievable how life is fragile; one mistake, or something you forget to do, can cost you your life and the life of others as well.

When the detector was properly plugged in and with batteries as a backup, I told my wife that is the reason my sister came to me the other day with the warning to be careful in the kitchen.

It all makes sense now that I think about it. I am convinced it was her that shoved me to wake me up. If this is not proof that our loved ones are watching over us, I do not know what is.

She basically saved both our lives. I will never forget this close call for as long as I live. In my prayers, I let her know that I was grateful for what she did. If I make it to heaven, the first thing that I am going to do is give you a big hug. Thank you for keeping an eye on your dumb brother.

It was very difficult for me to write about that evening. I must admit, it made me shed a few tears, after all, contrary to what people believe I am only human. A friend came over, he wanted me to go visit the house he purchased and moved in several weeks ago. He was certain that the house was haunted.

"Why did you not call me instead of driving over here? It would have saved you the time and trouble to come to get me to go to your place. You're lucky I was home."

"Yes, I know. I was afraid that if I called, you would have said no because of all the shit and people you deal with."

"This is different from who you are, my friend. I know that you would not call for some stupid thing that does not make any sense. I am curious to see what is going on with the paranormal in your house. You know there is not much that I can do."

"I know, I want you to witness for yourself what I am dealing with because you deal with ghosts and spirits."

"It's not the same. I have a question for you before buying your place, did you do a background check? Do a little research on the history of the property. You know, previous owners and all that stuff to make sure that you were not purchasing a house full of problems."

"Not really."

"What do you mean, not really?"

"I asked a few questions to the real estate agent."

"The agents will not divulge any unnecessary information; certainly nothing negative about the house. Did the agent lead you to believe that it was a good place… you know a good fit for you and your family? They want to close the deal as quickly as possible just in case some information would pop up that could prevent the selling of the house."

"Now that you mentioned it, she was fast at closing the sale."

"Like I said, they work fast with minimum information as possible. They are not looking out for you, all they want is the commission and move on to the next house."

"I guess you are right. She was in a hurry to close the sale."

"They work as fast as speedy Gonzales in the bugs bunny cartoons."

"Have you ever heard of a Mister Thomas that used to live on the outskirts of town?"

"I cannot say that I do."

"You know, the old two-story white house about five minutes from town. If you are going east, the house is on your left about fifty feet from the highway."

"Yes, I know which house you're talking about. The house has been abandoned for at least ten years.

"I know I got the house, dirt cheap. It needs a little bit of TLC and my being a connoisseur in carpentry, I will be able to do the repairs myself."

"When you told me you were in the market to buy a house, I assumed you would take your time to buy a house in town, not jump for joy and purchase the first house you saw."

"I know but I was in a hurry. The day after purchasing my future home, I took the plane to go work my final week with the company. We moved in a couple of weeks ago."

We turn into the driveway.

"This, my friend, is our new home. When we go in the house, you can hear a humming sound coming from upstairs."

"Are you sure it is not a problem with the plumbing, maybe a light fixture?"

"No, I double checked everything. I can guarantee you my friend, it has nothing to do with the plumbing or anything else for that matter."

"When the house is quiet, we can hear a noise coming from the den. A sound that someone is dragging a chair on the floor and then sitting down. The kids are scared. We all sleep in the same room."

"I have to admit, the humming sound is annoying."

"Can you stay long enough to hear the noise in the den?"

"Tonight, I will go in the den to observe what is really happening."

His wife was happy to hear that I was going to stay until evening and spend some time in the den.

"Thank you. Your friend is too much of a scary cat to go take a look."

I called my wife to let her know I would be late coming home. As the night approached, I made my way to the den, sat in a corner and waited, almost dozing off a few times. After waiting for a couple of hours, my patience paid off. I was able to hear the grinding of the chair being dragged on the floor and someone park his ass in the chair.

I was exiting what my pal called the"horror chamber". My friend was waiting at the door.

"So did you hear the fracas?"

"The what?"

"The noise."

"Yes, I did. You are already aware that I cannot do anything to remedy the situation. Regrettably sometimes, you have to deal with the circumstances of buying an old house particularly if you do not do your homework before buying."

"Yes, I know. You have told me about a dozen times today about not doing a background check. I don't need to hear it anymore. I get it for god's sake."

"Alright, I am sorry. You can bless the house by reciting prayers, cleanse every room in the house with sage, ask the entities to leave by saying they do not belong here anymore. It is no longer their house; it is my house."

He called me several days later to say nothing worked.

"Like I said, there is nothing that I can do; it is not my field of expertise. What you need is the help of a priest and a paranormal investigator."

"It's going to cost me money. They certainly do not do it for free?"

"I do not know I do not deal in these sorts of things."

The talk about costing them money when I advise people to seek help elsewhere is always negative. I feel used, individuals want me to take care of their dilemma for free.

A couple of days after our conversation, his wife finally convinced him to call an expert to get rid of the ghosts, haunting their home. The paranormal investigator and the priest were able to chase the spirits out of the house. Apparently, there are no more disturbances.

Chapter 18

At home, we can always feel a cool breeze and then hear a knock when entering the bathroom. I am certain that it is an entity that was given the shitty task to annoy us, or he was not doing his duty as a devil's disciples and simply wanted to dispose of him or flush him out of their group.

Either that he has the runs or he has a constipation problem. I personally think that he is full of shit. Well, anyway, if he keeps residing in the bathroom, he will have to dish out some cash for room and board. All kidding aside, he is very irritating, you always have the sensation of being watched. It just dawned on me that he is a pervert.

You cannot do your business without being nervous that he might manifest when you're sitting on porcelain betty. If he does make his presence known while on the can or taking a shower, we could be in a bad predicament. That is what you call"caught with your pants down".

A speculation, a theory floating around that I might be from alien descent or was abducted and they gave me special powers. Maybe I am one of the aliens that is living on earth concealing my identity disguised like a human. I could be an alien spy-- watching every move the humans make.

A few years ago, a couple of days before a full moon, a fellow would follow my every step. One night, I tricked him and I was able to corner him.

"Let's talk. For the past few months now, when there is a full moon, you pop up watching me. Can you explain to me what you are snooping for?"

"I am curious if you change shapes when there is a full moon."

"Wow! Are you for real? You took on quite the challenge to spy on me. I see that you have a camera, any interesting photos that I would have the privilege and the honor of sharing with you? "

"No, not yet."

"Not yet, really? Are you alone on your hunt to scoop up dirt on me or are there others like you from the nut house roaming the streets? Did you escape or did they release you from their care?"

"Only me."

"That's a shame; no one else wanted to join you in your glorious, illustrious escapade. They could become famous tagging along with you. I can see the headlines, so you came up with this idea all by yourself."

"Magazines or newspapers pay good money for a good story especially one like mine."

"I am at loss for words, you should be extremely proud of yourself. I can bet a month salary that your camera has been idle since starting this important mission."

"My camera is ready to take pictures."

"The reason you cannot take pictures. I wait until I get home around midnight, and I turn into a flesh-eating monster. The werewolves are afraid of me. That is why people keep disappearing without a trace. After midnight, I snatch them in their sleep and never to be found again. There are thousands of us."

He was standing a few feet away from me, with his mouth wide open with nothing to say.

"Be on your toes, aliens are looking for bimbos like you to conduct sexual experiments. Too bad, the scientists do not know you.

They would be astonished just by looking at you. Now that you know, I cannot let you go."

I made my way towards him.

"Boo."

"You are mocking me."

"Yes, I am! Put it in your pipe and smoke it."

"I don't smoke."

"I still do not know how people like you can get through life… I mean, come on! Hiding in bushes with a camera in case I change shapes on a full moon. What do you do for a living?"

"I am on social assistance."

"Of course, you are. Be warned, if I catch you stalking me again, I am going to kick your ass to kingdom come. You get the drift."

"Understood."

"Go home now before I turn into a ferocious beast… grab you, bring you to my lair and barbecue you for dinner tonight. You will become another statistic of missing people."

As I watched him leave,

"What a blockhead, a waste of a good soul. He is not the sharpest tool in the shed."

Another inquiry that comes up quite often is: if I walk in heaven with the souls, Can I take pictures and talk about the scenery? I wish I could, you only walk in heaven when you pass away. I guide the souls towards the light, I never go any further. Some individuals wanted me to take a polygraph test. Some call it a lie detector test. Me, I call it rubbish. How can a machine detect when you are lying?

As an indigo child, I am able to see both sides of human beings-- the good and the bad. I am surprised how people can be mean and selfish. There will always be souls that are confused… or lost on the highway of life. Some get off the highway to take back roads that end up in dead ends.

Some souls do not want to go because of unfulfilled opportunities. When they die, they do not know where to turn. They become vulnerable and the dark side pounces, lures them into hell. That is where I come in.

My friend who owns a welding company made a steel cross for me to help protect myself from further attacks. He did a very good job; very nice, welded steel shaped like a cross with pointed, sharp ends. A bit on the heavy side to carry in my pockets but, what a great idea.

I do not know why the idea of a steel cross never crossed my mind. Father Joseph blessed my new cross with holy water. I now have a new weapon to help me defend myself. One night when we came home from visiting friends, as we entered the house, my wife said,

"Can you hear what I am hearing?"

At first, I shook my head but after carefully listening, I was able to hear the beat of native drums.

"I can hear native drums.

"Yes, it is precisely what I am hearing."

"My elders are trying to relay some kind of warning."

I was able to see a silhouette in the shape of a human being with feathers in his hands. He proceeded on waving the feathers. My elders came to warn me that there were several evil entities in the house ready to do battle. I bowed my head to show that I understood. The beat of the drums stopped and my elder vanished. I said to my wife,

"Let's go back outside for a minute."

I advised her of what was about to go down.

"Understood."

"Let's go in and oust our unwanted squatters."

We went back in the house, and everything was eerily quiet. We checked every room in the house including the basement... nothing. We both parked our carcass on the couch and started watching television. One hour goes by... then two, and still nothing. Maybe a false alarm, which I doubt because my elders are never wrong when it comes to the paranormal... or maybe the entities vacated the premises.

When it was time to go to bed, all hell broke loose. I saw four black entities in the hallway, all four came at me. I yelled to my wife,

"Go get my new cross. It's on the kitchen table and toss it to me."

All four were inflicting pain in my lower abdomen. My wife threw a strike right down the middle of the plate. She was right on the money. I was able to grab the cross with one hand and I stabbed one of the entities.

He let out a very loud growl and vanished in thin air. His compadres also followed suit. When I stabbed the entity, the cross pierced the body of the malevolent spirit.

As I limped back to my chair

"Thank god for my new cross."

"Are you all right?"

"Yes, some pain in my abdomen but nothing to worry about."

You could distinctly see some redness. I could feel a little bit of a burning sensation. My wife said,

"Go look in the mirror."

Looking in the mirror I could see numerous small symbols engraved on my belly. The scoundrels waited to lurk in the shadows setting up an ambush. I will say it again, 'thank god for my new cross'. Also, many thanks to my dear friend for providing me with a new weapon.

They were out for blood. I went into the bathroom to wash my face. When I took a second peek in the mirror, I saw the devil's face instead of mine. I shook my head, and I took another peek. To my relief, it was my face. As for the satanic symbols on my belly, it stands for evil, and it is used to conjure evil spirits. I rubbed the symbols with holy water, which took care of the burning sensation.

After a few weeks with no further attacks, the symbols were no longer visible. I did not inform Father Joseph about the attack. I need to learn to resolve some issues on my own. One night, my wife disrupted my sleep.

"Take a look at my legs. You are scratching my legs with your toenails and also making funny noises."

"You have to be kidding me."

"I am not kidding. Look at the scratch marks on my legs. You are scratching me with your toenails."

I did not know what to say.

"For the last few nights now, you scratch me while you are asleep."

"Why did you not let me know before tonight?"

"At first, it was only a few scratches. The following night... again, only a few scratches. But tonight, a totally new ball game. The scratching was getting more intense that is why I woke you up."

"What the hell is going on? I am taken aback. I know for a fact I am not dreaming when the scratching occurs. After breakfast tomorrow morning, I will call Father Joseph to see what he makes of all this."

The next morning after talking to Father Joseph, he came over to the house to take a look at the wounds on my wife's legs.

"Goodness! Look at that."

We went into the kitchen and over a cup of coffee he told me

"The devil's warriors have found a way to manifest in your dreams."

"If it's happening while I am dreaming, I would remember because I told my wife that I was not dreaming. It's strange for me to have no recollection."

"Sometimes, dreams are like sleepwalking. Remember the night you found yourself in the snowbank? They wait until you are in a deep sleep to enter your dreams.

"Sneaky assholes."

"About ninety percent of people who dream when in a deep sleep do not recollect dreaming. Before going to bed, pray and ask your guardian angel to stand guard and when they show up to chase them away."

"I am confused Father. We determined that my sleepwalking was because of the collision in a dimension."

"We did not come to that conclusion with speculation that it might not be the case. We also said that it might be just a coincidence."

"I am sorry for my confusion. The thought of hurting my wife while I sleep is a big concern for me."

"No need to apologize, I can certainly understand. Well, I have to go. If you need me, you know where to find me."

"I certainly will. I have your number on speed dial."

As a precaution, for a week I slept in the guest room. I was worried I might cause my wife more harm. The first night when I slept in our bed, my wife could not sleep-- she was nervous. I don't blame her.

I suggested that maybe it would be wise for me to sleep in the guest room for a little while longer. She said, no, she wanted me to sleep by her side. The night was peaceful. The scratching is over. Bizarre, but good, it was only for a few nights. This is a real head-scratcher trying to decipher the reason why it happened.

One question that pops up quite often, "if I know where to find the holy grail, I wish I did but no". The location has never been revealed to anyone. Legends tell the story that the holy grail has not been seen since Jesus had last supper with his disciples.

There are many revelations when it comes to the holy grail. Jesus was the last person to drink from the holy grail. It has been hidden for the purpose of: No one else would be able to drink from that precious cup. Who knows? The mystery dates back to the Middle Ages. Apparently, rumors have it that it is in the hands of an underground society.

One evening, I was at my favorite restaurant enjoying a nice dinner with my wife. When another customer spotted me. He commenced bad-mouthing me. He once asked me a few questions that I did not have the answers. He thinks that I am a guru. I told my wife,

"I will be back in a few minutes."

"What are you going to do?"

"Nothing to worry about."

I joined him at his table.

"So you have been bad-mouthing me now for about fifteen minutes nonstop, with some disgusting comments. Do you kiss your mother with that dirty mouth of yours?"

"Say what, I am only telling the truth."

"People come here to have a nice dinner with family and friends. They do not want to hear your blabbermouth and repulsive comments about me. Do you think that I am a walking dictionary or a book to you?"

"No, it's not like that."

"If you would take the time to read books and surf the internet, you might find what you are looking for or… are you too stupid to do that?"

"I am not dumb."

"If you can read, there would be no need to ask questions and presume I have the answer. I am not a mountain of knowledge. If I do not have the answers you're looking for then there is no need to put me down like you are doing right now."

"I am only stating a fact."

"Reading books would prevent you from being flustered and frustrated. Stop assuming that I will be able to help you. If you do not like what you hear, do not ask for information. Now, I would advise you to shut your trap. You're polluting the place."

"OK, OK, OK… for crying out loud."

"I think that you are a lazy, stupid, ignorant son of a bitch; but I will keep it to myself and… Oh yes! You are also very ugly. If you do not shut up, you will be eating soup from a straw for the next six months."

He gulped down his meal and went out the door. We were able to finish our dinner without having to listen to jabber jaws. A good majority of the population thinks or assumes that I take drugs every day; that I am always high on different drugs powerful enough for me to have hallucinations or hear voices......

A group of volunteers held an event to help generate financial support for a charity with a fifties and sixties party. Back then, the wardrobe for men was jeans, a white t-shirt, and a leather jacket. Smokers would tuck their smokes inside their t-shirt in between their biceps and the shoulder. Everybody dressed for the occasion.

The buffet dinner was delicious. It was followed by an evening dance. I was waiting in line for my turn to serve myself at the buffet table when one of my friends says for fun.

"Is that a pack of cigarettes you have tucked away in your t-shirt?"

A guy that I despise because of his attitude was also waiting in line interjected our conversation with his comments.

"We all know that pack contains drugs."

I grabbed him by the throat rammed him in the coat rack.

"Listen, pipsqueak. Vermons such as yourself start rumors and talk behind people's back. If you ever say anything like that again, you will pay the price for opening that big mouth of yours. I will put my feet in your face."

When I finally released my grip from his throat so that he could breathe again, I addressed the crowd by saying,

"Does anyone else have something to say?... No? Good. I am sorry for the disturbance but I cannot leave the house without being the target of some ludicrous comments thrown my way by clowns like him."

The little runt went home. Besides that ugly episode, I had an enjoyable evening. Easter Sunday, I always get a barrage of queries about the resurrection of Jesus Christ our savior like... if I have the privilege of witnessing Jesus coming out of his tomb, or if I am able to communicate with saints? No, I cannot do both queries. One thing that I know.

I am talking by experience, easter water always stays fresh no matter how long before you make use of it. For easter water, you have to go where there is running water, like a creek. You have from midnight until dawn to go and fill your containers with easter water.

Do you know that we are coded at birth? We are destined to have certain potential and excel at certain things. It is hard to believe as I myself did not know until my near death while swimming. Many in the world are unaware of this as well.

(*Celestial saying: Each one of us is beautiful and unique individual being capable of more than we think. Sometimes, the problem is finding clues in what we are capable of and tap into the potential of your cosmic powers. Crack open the door a little at a time and see your life make a quantum leap forward. We are all magic; our soul is a giant beam of light and every specific purpose you came to this earth.*)

Your guardian angel will always be your number one friend; stands by you in good or bad times. He will continue to guide you through life and will never let you down. There are no accidents in the universe. Every major event in your life has happened for a reason.

Chapter 19

The years have caught up to me. It takes me more time to get back in the saddle after a confrontation and move forward. I was struggling for a while both mentally and physically. I started reciting prayers every day for reinforcements. Again, my elders answered the call.

I began to see feathers in front of me. They rescued me with the use of my beliefs, spirituality by sending messages from their souls to my soul. It clarified so many thoughts in my brain. I am not stuck in quicksand anymore. I can move forward again.

The messages made me understand that what we do in life echoes in eternity and not to underestimate myself. I know more than I say, think more than I speak, and notice more than I realize.

It made me go back to restart my brain which was in neutral to find my spiritual folders. It brought me back to reality-- whatever you do or say, there are always consequences and not to dwell on issues that I cannot change.

For me, it was the boost I needed to gather my thoughts to keep going. It was a real eye-opener. I flushed my brain from all the crap that was slowing me down. One of the reasons for the decline in my life.

I was having difficulty chasing away a pesky, noisy entity that made my basement his home. It was a heck of a fight to evict him from the house. In a way, I do not blame him. He was enjoying the fact that he was getting free rent.

Me renting the hall to educate the population was of no purpose. People still have the mentality embedded in their skulls; that I am able to do everything under the sun. On occasions, the information that I provided to a sibling ends in a family squabble.

One night, I was able to see a full body apparition of one of my elders. He was reciting a native spiritual prayer to me, making gestures with his hands. The motion of his hands was sending positive vibes my way. His visit was short. As soon as he finished his ritual, he was gone. Since that night, so far so good. Things have been quiet in the house.

One day coming out of the bank, I was shoved by a man who wanted to beat me up. He was going to make me eat my words what I told his mom. I gave his mother false hope for his dad.

"About six months ago, you told my mom that my father would be cured. Do you remember talking to her?"

He was looking at me with poisonous darts in his eyes.

"I listened to what you had to say. Now, it is my turn to speak. Who the hell are you? What is the name of your mother?"

"Her name is Elda. The name of my dad is Henry. Do you recollect now or you rather not remember? I want an answer."

"Backup the truck for a moment. I did not catch everything that you just said. You're talking a mile a minute. One thing that I cannot stand is a prick like you in my face trying to frighten me."

He was looking at me and shaking his head.

"So, park your attitude at the door. Change your frame of mind or I will change it for you. I vaguely remember her. Anyway, I always advise people what I see."

He interrupted me.

"You lie to people."

"As I was saying, I always advise the individual that comes to see me that things could change. I have no control over that."

I attempted several times to reason with him. He would not listen. He pushed me again. It was obvious that he wanted to fight. I landed a lucky punch on the side of his thick head, knocking him out cold. By then, there was a small group of rubberneckers that gathered to watch the fight. Some were saying, *'Good for you. He deserved it'.*

Another bystander said,

"I would give him a few more."

The knucklehead was getting back up. He glanced at me picked up his hat got into his car and drove away. Another bystander yelled.

"Go crawl back in your hole that you came from."

Harsh words but good. One of my very best and dearest friends, he was more than a brother to me, passed away. When we were dispatched to my friend's address, I did not go. I knew he was not going to make it.

It would have been too painful for me to see him on a stretcher fighting for his life. He died of a heart attack. I waited at the command post until the guys came back. I wanted to read the medical report.

I wanted to remember his smiling face instead of the one in distress. On the eve of his funeral, he was in my dreams to let me know that he was at peace and not to fret over his passing and keep the memories alive.

We worked, played sports, fish, coached little league, hung out together. The morning of his funeral, I was having flashbacks of the happy moments we spent together. He was a very good and honest person. He was one of the best.

The church was packed ready to burst at the seams. He touched a lot of people volunteering for a lot of organizations. People wanted to say a final goodbye. It was very moving and touching moment. I could see his spirit over his casket.

Some spirits attend their own funerals to make sure they have a good resting place. Some funerals that I attended while in church; some mourners smiled at me, some looked at me with a weird look or gave me the evil eye. I always sit at the back, in the church. I never stay to chat. I might gather an unwanted crowd and disrupt the celebration of life of the deceased.

A friend of a friend was deer hunting. At the end of the day, he could not find his way back to his truck. Darkness was fast approaching. He was not sure which direction he should take. When you are lost in the woods no matter which direction you look, the outlines of the forest all look the same. The sky was pitch black-- no stars, no moonlight.

He decided to take an old beaten trail. He was anxious to get out of his predicament. He kept walking using his flashlight for guidance. He came upon some sort of sacrificial, worshipping site. He decided to settle in for the night, trying to get as comfortable as possible. The next morning, he took the same trail as the night before. The trail was a large beaten path with a lot of foot traffic.

When he finally found the road, he was able to find his truck. He drove to my friend's house to tell him what he discovered the previous night. Of course, my friend suggested coming over to my house and have a chat about the site. They proposed that I go with them to take a closer look.

"I am not interested to go take a look. The site does not concern me, what ever goes on over there is none of my concern and none of my business. Leave it alone. You might be opening a can of worms by going back and snoop around."

"You're the perfect guy to come with us because of what you are capable to do. We need your wisdom."

"You want my wisdom, then leave it alone. If you are so intrigued on finding something, talk to the cops. They will investigate to find out what really goes on in that neck of the woods."

A couple of days later, two cops knocked on my door. I took a deep breath and thinking, '*not again, what now?*' I let them in.

"It came to our attention that there may be some kind of worshipping going on not far from here."

"I know, the friend of a friend came upon the area where there might be some ceremonies to worship the devil. I advised him to go talk to the police."

"He did come to us that is why I am here today. Are you involved in any of that stuff?"

"Not again, this is getting ridiculous. I did have a conversation with a fellow geez. I do not know, maybe a year ago. He tried to recruit me to join his clan of worshippers."

"What did you tell him."

"I let him know that he was crazy and to stop bothering me. I know they have a place where they meet every month, but I do not know the location. They can shove their rituals up where the sun does not shine. I am sick and tired that my name is always dragged in the mud when it comes to that kind of hogwash."

"If we get a warrant to search your dwelling, you know your residence."

"I know what dwelling means."

"Will we find evidence that you are involved in all of this?"

"No need for a warrant. Go ahead, come in and search the house."

"We cannot do a search without a warrant signed by a judge. If we find evidence without a warrant, it will not be allowed in court. Is that what you are trying to do by telling us we could do the search right now?"

"No, of course not. I have nothing to hide."

"Why then would they think that you would be involved?"

"Boy, if these walls could talk, you would have your answer. I have no clue why and I… Frankly, I do not want to know. I do not give a rat's ass about what goes on over there. If you need an answer, go interrogate the bunch of… I do not even know how to call those lunatics anymore."

I took a couple of deep breaths.

"I have no words to describe, or what I think of the individuals that once again mentioned my name. I should launch a lawsuit for harassment or defamation of character. Maybe then they would leave me alone."

The cops said.

"We can understand your frustration but keep in mind, we might have to come back to search the house."

"I don't like it, but I understand."

"OK, then we will be on our way. Enjoy the rest of the day."

"Well, of course. I will enjoy the rest of my day especially after an episode like this one."

Man, what a nightmare of people with nothing between the ears, put me through. I am sure that if they go for a brain scan, the doctors would only be able to see an air tunnel between the ears, nothing else. When my wife came home I told her about the nice visit earlier in the afternoon.

"Again."

"Yes, again. Sweety."

"I am flabbergasted with all of this. It's really getting on my nerves, and I am starting to lose patience with all the bozos in this world."

"Yes, I know honey."

Some citizens from town suggested that I should open a store where you can buy… like they said, weird stuff. A store somewhat like the voodoo stores that you see on T.V. One individual mentioned he was in New Orleans, Louisiana and purchased a few items from a voodoo store that sold all kinds of weird stuff.

Louisiana is a state where a good portion of the population believe or practice witchcraft; that is why voodoo stores are thriving. Around here is a totally different story. I would be lucky to sell a few items a week.

I appreciate the suggestion, but I have too many things on my plate as it is. I do not want to sell any of that stuff. Customers are asking a ton of questions. A never-ending curiosity from the public and maybe causing an uproar from people not wanting a voodoo store in their neighborhood or community. I already have a job.

Their indication is that I would make a fortune because I have knowledge of that kind of stuff.

"People like to buy out-of-this-world objects."

"How do you know? Have you conducted a survey? If you did, I would like to see the results."

"Your store would attract customers from every walk of life."

"I do not see why not that any of you could not open a store. Like you said, there is a lot of money to be made."

I get calls like this one. A man was looking to buy demon fighting supplies from me or if I could point him in the right direction where he could purchase the ingredients. He needed to concoct a potion, because he was possessed by the devil and demons. He was upset that I could not procure him with what he needed to expel the demons inside of him.

Again, it was proposed by one of his friends to drop me a line that I would be able to help him. Again, I needed to reiterate that I did not deal with these types of circumstances. I told him to go talk to a priest.

"Do you know if he sells that kind of stuff?"

"I have no idea. You will have to ask him." I gave him Father Joseph's phone number and wished him good luck.

Many nosy individuals want to know if I see Jesus every time I guide a soul. First, it was inquiries about Easter and now, questions if I see Jesus while I fulfill my duty. So far, only once did I was able to get a visual of Jesus while travelling in different dimensions. He was holding a young child in his arms. He put the child down. The little one was running around him with his arms wide open.

Jesus was surrounded by a white mist. He quickly glanced at me, bowed his head, his lips where moving. I was not close enough to hear what he was talking about. He lifted his head to look at me again and placed both arms to his chest. The inside of his hands towards me.

An aura was forming around him. He lowered his head and did not move his hands. Angels formed a circle around me. Smiling, he took another quick peek at me and extended his arms in my direction. I could feel the sensation of being hit in the chest by a bolt of lightning. He did a ninety-degree turn with his back at me and walked away.

The white aura around him doubled in size. The angels made their way to be by his side. Father Joseph had those comments about me making eye contact with Jesus.

"Jesus cleansed you to help you with the entities that keep invading your home. I hope you understand that the entities will not put an end to ruining your days or evenings. It's like giving you one extra tool-- the stamina needed to tackle the nasty beings from the dark side, that persist to be a torn in your side."

"I wish I could make them disappear for good."

"I hear you, my friend."

I get letters in the mail by people who envy me to be able to do what I do. Some wish for the power to cure sick people. For some, if they could foresee what the future holds for them, and make the world a better place.

I never write back to the senders. What's the use if they never comprehend how serious the events can be. Are they ready to devote themselves to the things that needs to be done? Good or bad, the letters always go directly to the recycle bin. I was in a restaurant having lunch, a man I barely know joined me at my table.

"Do you mind if I sit down?"

He was seated before I could answer.

"Are you aware how lucky you are to possess such a gift? I wish I could trade everything that I own so that I could have unlimited powers to be able to control people's destiny."

"You want to control people's destiny; no one should be able to control someone's destiny. It is up to the individual to control his or her own journey, not you."

"That is what I keep on wishing for."

"What foolishness. What would you part with or trade to gain such power?"

"I am willing to part with everything I own; even my soul."

"You know, with power comes great responsibility. You should be more cautious for what you wish for. Someone might be paying attention, listening for what you want."

"I am not worried."

It so happened that a malevolent entity was eavesdropping on our conversation. A few days after our conversation, I got a phone call. The caller was Mr. wish everything for power on the phone.

"It's me... you know, from the restaurant."

"Yes, the one that was willing to give up everything for power."

"Yes, that's me. Remember when I told you about my wish? You told me to be careful what I wish for, like you said someone might be listening. Someone was indeed listening. A demon came to me and said, '*I can give you the power that you seek for one condition: You would be devoted to me for all eternity, alive and dead.*'"

"What did you say? Did you agree to his proposal?"

"Gosh, no! I will never wish for that nonsense ever again."

"I hope so, for your sake. You were a man with a blindfold, trying to find new adventures without knowing where you would end up, and suffer the consequences that it might bring."

"Yes, I know."

"You were really gung-ho about obtaining powers. Do not be surprised if he comes back to try to convince you to change your mind. They detest the word *no*."

"He is always around, hounding me."

"I do not want to alarm you, but he will be relentless… nonstop in his pursuit until he is able to snatch your soul."

"Do you really think so?"

"I know so. You went fishing and the biggest fish in the pond took the bait. He wants to get in your boat. Are you Catholic?"

"Yes, I am."

"If I were you, I would go to church. Ask god to forgive you and to provide you with the help you will need to chase the demon away. Also, seek help from the church because he will not let go of his stranglehold, he now has on you. He will not be patient for long."

"Jesus! I did not know it could be that bad."

"He will destroy you to get what he wants. I do not want to be pessimistic; chances are, you might not survive his assault. When you hang up the phone, do not waste another minute go see a priest. He will be able to help you and get things in motion to get that entity off your back."

"OK. I will do that ASAP."

Even with the help of a priest, the entity was still holding on to him. The demon was a fierce warrior, not willing to surrender. Finally with the help of an archbishop, they were able to remove the chokehold the demon had on the poor fellow.

I hope he has learned his lesson not to wish for unrealistic, dangerous rubbish that could cause him grief or even his life. We are supposed to learn from our mistakes. I sure hope he learned his lesson.

Entities, demons, dark spirits, fallen angels or whatever you choose to call them, they all do the same trying to suck the life out of you. They will use any tactic in the book that's why they lurk in the dark while we sleep, when we are the most vulnerable, and do their best work preparing an ambush for you.

It does not matter if you are sleeping or awake; they will pounce, and blindside you. They use the element of surprise with no chances for you to react and defend yourself. They always wait for you to be in a compromising position and catch you with your pants down.

If you are having problems with one or more spirits in your home, I would not hesitate to wager one year's pay. They are mostly active at night. Take the necessary precautions. Do not give them any slack because if you do, their presence will increase.

There is a big chance that they will either attach themselves to or possess you. The demon will have complete power over your poor soul by manifesting through your speech and in what you do.

The person who is possessed is in for a whole lot of hurt and may carry emotional and physical scars for the rest of his or her life. They will first make their presence known to the children because they are vulnerable-- easy to control.

If you notice a dramatic change in the attitude of your child; if he talks about a new friend or monster in the house... be careful. It could be the beginning of something very sinister. Seek help as soon as possible.

(Quote from the Pope: *Don't argue with the devil, he's much more intelligent than us. Satan is a very smart person. He wants to divide and conquer every man for himself. The devil takes the end most, telling everyone they should look after themselves and not care about others.*)

It has been a couple of weeks since a silhouette caught my eye. A male ghost watching me from a distance. His attire is a white shirt and brown pants. When I try to get closer to get a better look, he evaporates in thin air.

Every day, he does his daily ritual like clockwork. It does not matter where I am; he is always aware of my whereabouts. Maybe he planted a tracking device somewhere on my body.

I have no clue what he wants and why he is keeping an eye on me. I am at wits end. I am bursting my brain as to why he is keeping his distance. It is driving me nuts not knowing. I have a notion to leave him a note that I am no good at long distance relationships.

I wonder if it's words or inappropriate language that came out of my mouth. Maybe I was supposed to do something or did something that offended someone. Maybe he is standing guard in case I do something that is not appropriate that would hurt someone. He does not look menacing. All he does is look at me until I try to approach him. He does his disappearing act.

It's freaky… I wonder how long he will keep admiring me. Maybe he is a magician that passed away and he wants to show me his disappearing trick? He could be relaying messages or warnings to someone or something. As long as he does not cause me any headaches, there is nothing much that I can do. I am hoping that he will get bored and leave me alone and never come back.

My wife cannot see him. He makes himself visible only to me. I tried yelling, waving at him, no reaction. It has been a couple of frustrating months. It's been a few days now since I last saw him. I hope that this baloney of watching me has ended.

Still, a mystery for me. Everything is still up in the air. What was his purpose? I hope he stays away. The suspense might not be over. Stay tuned do not change the channel he might make another appearance.

I am keeping my fingers, toes crossed in case he decides to come back to again keep me in the fog as to what he wants. Maybe a demon spy? Maybe he has a crush on me, or I am very popular in the underworld and wanted my autograph and was too shy to ask? I guess I will never know.

One evening, I was walking to my truck. I detected a beast in the middle of the road making his way towards me. If my memory does not deceive me, it was close to ten pm. I live on a dead end street with only six houses.

Everything was quiet until I noticed that thing walking in my direction. He came to a halt under the streetlight in front of my house. The distance between us was maybe fifty feet. At first, I took a quick glance at the creature. I stopped dead in my tracks.

He was standing under the streetlight. I had a good vision of what he looked like. I am sure that he was not coming over to introduce himself and shake my hand. He was the most horrifying creature that I have ever seen.

I have watched many horror movies based on true events, but he takes the cake. I have never seen anything that even resembled anything close to the life form across the street.

After a brief stop under the light, he started making his way towards me. I froze and I could not move. I know that I mentioned on numerous occasions that nothing would scare me. I guess you should never say never. I locked horns with the devil a few times but never anything like this beast.

Green eyes and about six feet tall; he was humongous-- about the same size of a lineman in the national football league. Liquid was coming out of his nose. A very large mouth. With his green eyes, you could feel that he was able to see right through you.

A greyish color, which seemed to be dead skin all over his body. Short arms, but no hands, only long fingers. No feet, only toes, and no horns. From what I could observe, no ears. There was something on his back and I could not quite make out what it was. We locked eyes for a brief moment. I could see some kind of movement on his back. A set of small red eyes came into view.

The small creature jumped off from his shoulders. He began trotting in my direction. I was about ten feet from my truck, when I was finally able to move. I hurried like a bat out of hell to reach my truck. I could not run fast enough; as if I was moving in slow motion.

Once in the truck, I turned on the headlights. I was able to have a clear view of the small entity. He was shaped like a miniature devil. The distance between us was closing fast. I floored it and I put the pedal to the metal. I wanted to lose him, leaving him and his little buddy in the dust. My heart was beating out of my chest. I peeked in the rearview mirror.

They were giving chase running like crazy behind the truck. I turned into the church's parking lot, and hurried to get inside Father Joseph's residence. He was surprised to see me running into his house. He inquired.

"Are you all right?"

I was still catching my breath when I replied.

"No."

"What is going on? It must be very serious. I have never seen you before in this state of mind. Someone or something really rattled your chain. My dear Lord, what is wrong?"

After catching my breath and be able to speak.

"Can you please come outside with me?"

Both creatures were standing near my truck and a short distance from Father Joseph's front door. He was mesmerized by what he was looking at. I can still, to this day, remember the look on his face. A face of fear filled with confusion.

"What are they? What is their purpose? What do they want to accomplish by following you here?"

The beast and his little buddy wanted us to see their presence by not moving an inch while we were outside. I suggested that we should go back inside.

"I cannot express the way I feel. I do not know what to say. I am speechless. I have never laid eyes before on something so frightening in my entire life."

"I can understand why you bolted into the house in such a hurry."

"What can we do?"

"We have no choice; we need to face them and try to find out what they want and chase them away."

We stepped outside. They were still in the same spot; they did not budge an inch. They were standing there like statues. We were descending the steps proceeding with caution when Father Joseph stopped for a few seconds.

"We need to go back inside."

It was like, I was stuck in the middle of a horror movie; unable to fast forward to the end of the movie. Our predicament was getting tense with every passing seconds. We were both nervous. The reason Father Joseph wanted to retreat to the house was because he was able to get a better glimpse of the entities. Once inside, he blurted out.

"Oh my gosh."

He hurried to fetch a book. He shuffled a few pages.

"Come here and take a look at the picture in page twenty-two."

I thoroughly scrutinized the photo, I turned towards Father Joseph.

"Is this for real?"

"It's a photo of the creature outside in the parking lot. You're looking at a photo of the reincarnation demon."

"Reincarnation demon?"

"Yes, reincarnation demon. I heard about him. Until today, I thought, he only existed in tall tales. A fictitious character, a figment of imagination. Boy, what a wakeup call for me. Wow, wow, wow!"

I was totally confused and looked at Father Joseph.

"He was able to find is way here to cause havoc."

"There are motorists going back and forth. No one seems to notice him. How come?"

"He is invisible to the ones he does not have to deal with. Well, aren't we the lucky ones we get to have a very interesting interaction with the beast and his little partner?"

"Man! What an ugly dude."

Father Joseph gathered a few things and again, out the door we went. He shouted to the entity.

"You and the little midget, have no right to be here. This is the house of god, so remove your ugly carcasses from the holy ground that you are standing on."

Nothing, they did not even move a muscle. He repeated the same words over and over while slowly approaching the entities. We were maybe the length of a school bus before we could meet face to face, a thing I hoped would not materialize to see him face to face. The little one jumped off the creature, ran towards me and hit me in the ribs.

He was fast as lightning. He clobbered me before I had a chance to react, and he disappeared. The big ugly stinking one made a move in my direction. Father Joseph was reciting words from God.

When the demon was close enough, Father Joseph tossed a crucifix in his face. Before doing us a favor by going his own way, the beast pushed me to the ground. I was afraid that he might jump on me. He gazed at me, his face four feet from mine. He screamed and he was gone.

We went back inside, I said.

"Boy, what an encounter."

Father Joseph replied.

"We did battle with the reincarnation demon. In my mind, until today, I did not know that he really existed. For me, he was the subject of tall tales. He is the one that keeps patrolling for souls that are willing and ready to take another crack at life on earth. I read about him in the book but I was sure it was all hearsay. He tries to nab the souls and escort them to hell."

"My ribs hurt like crazy, the little runt got me good. I do not understand why he would try to injure me."

"His purpose tonight was to frighten you and cause you physical harm. To inflict pain was also on his to-do list."

"I have nothing to do with souls coming back to earth."

"Well, in a way, yes you do. You guide the souls to heaven. You take away the demon's ability to swindle souls to their house. When souls are ready to take another shot at life in the jungle we live in, again they try to interfere with the process of reincarnation."

"Really, I have that big of an impact?"

"The demons are always on a mission to gather souls to please their master. The infamous satan himself. You make their tasks more laborious. The reason for our visitor tonight was to get you out of their way."

(Demons also referred to as reincarny catchers. Their purpose is to catch reincarnies and send them to hell.)

"Really? Wow!"

"The souls that you save could be residing in hell instead of heaven due to the number of souls that make it to the house of god. The reincarnation demon has his work cut out to deliver souls to his boss. With you out of the way, his job would be a lot simpler."

All I could say was,

"Wow! What type of precautions should I take to prevent that pain in the ass to not come back?"

"I am afraid that precautions will not help. If he comes back, we will not be able to use the same tactics from tonight. He will use different ruses that are more complex."

"OK then. Like I said before, I was under the assumption that I am a very popular guy when it comes to the underworld."

"Maybe but not in a good way. Stay alert and be careful."

"I will go home and try to put this episode behind me."

I opened the door to leave.

"Father, come here for a minute."

We were both looking at the same entities standing in the box of my truck. When we got close to the truck, they made themselves invisible again.

"Can you hear that?"

"Yes, they came back to infest your truck with creepy crawlers."

We took the garden hose to get rid of some of the insects until I could make my way to a car wash. I washed my truck and finally went home. I was on edge in case he decided to return.

For an extended period of time, I took the habit of checking over my shoulders. My wife was also concerned that he might show up for another round. If he does, I am prepared to pin him down like in wrestling, 1 2 3… match over.

Episodes like the one with the reincarnation devil are blowing me into orbit. It makes me wonder if it is time for me to walk away. It is now a challenge for me to remain calm, keep it together with daily dumb questions such as, *'Have you ever been drunk when spirits reach out to you?'*.

The answer is no. First of all, I have not touched a beer or consumed any liquor since the day I put an end to my drinking. I was intelligent enough to realize that when drunk, I could have done some serious blunders. It's been many moons without a drop of alcohol.

The damn creature and his little sidekick are always in the back of my mind. That pint size varmint is fast and powerful. When he struck me that night, he broke two of my ribs.

My devoted fan, who took the time to observe my every move for a couple of months is keeping his distance. I have not seen him since his last day on the job, to keep tabs on me. I hope neither one of them comes back. I could be in a whole lot of hurt if they return.

I am left-handed; what you call a southpaw, and an indigo child is foremost the reason why a majority of the population perceives me as a weirdo. I am also a retard. While in grade school, the teacher was determined for me and two others of my classmates to write with our right hand. Decades ago, if you were a lefty, you belonged to the devil.

My mom had to intervene. I was not learning anything. My fingers were black and blue when I came home from school. The teacher was constantly whacking me on the fingers with her ruler.

The moto for the school board was, we would be on the sidelines until we could write with our right hand. The mothers with left-handed kids, came together to pressure members of the school board to be lenient and change that discriminating rule.

It caused a lot of raucous after deliberating for a month. They finally threw the towel and changed the school's policy. A big and important victory for us and for all other left-handed students for years to come.

It was a coincidence for me to be an indigo child and also a lefty. Some of my fellow southpaws inquired, if being left-handed made them an indigo child. Some were relieved when I said no. For some, it was a letdown.

I told them to not be disappointed, it is no picnic being an indigo child. It comes with enormous pressure and responsibility; you must deal with the paranormal, which is a pain in the ass. Some understand and change their attitude for wanting to be like me. Some said, they wanted to be an elite child; believe me I am far from being elite. There is always a defiant bunch.

No matter what you say or try to do in order to change their minds, you cannot penetrate their thick skulls. You have to educate yourself for some confrontations from the public that sometimes, it's like pulling teeth to get them to understand that it is not like it seems.

Some individuals come talk to me with their mind already made up. I always say, why bother to talk to me if you are already convinced that no matter what I say, you will not change your point of view.

Chapter 20

I am afraid when I decide to retire from performing my duties as an indigo child. I am willing to bet the amount of money in my bank accord which is not much. When word gets out, I am calling it quits. The population will have a field day with a good variety of opinions or comments.

For example: you will miss the lifestyle that you have been living for so many years. In no time, I will go back to what I was doing. I will betray the ones who trust and rely on me. One fellow compared my decision; to hang up the gloves is like trying to quit smoking. You need at least two, three or more attempts before solemnly committing to get rid of your weakness for tobacco.

Some smokers call it dependance of the cancer sticks. They suffer from nicotine withdrawal. I will get bored out of my mind. I will suffer from daily routine withdrawal. To be honest, I did not know that there was such a thing as a routine withdrawal. You learn new things every day. That it is why, senior citizens are walking history and wisdom books.

I agree that it will be a challenge to remove myself from the public eye and call it a victory. Some smokers are successful in quitting smoking; some abandon. Too much of an effort to achieve their quest of living tobacco-free. For me, it is a totally different scenario. What I mean is, when you climb the tree of life and you reach the last branch, you have done your share.

It is the time to start contemplating retirement. That is exactly what is in store for me: to retire happy because I know that every day, I do my best. It will take a heavy load off that was glued to my shoulders for so many years. I admit that it is going to be strange-- a new way of life.

I advised Father Joseph about my intentions for the near future. I made him aware that I am not at the finish line yet but very close to finishing my marathon of my current way of living.

When done, I will start living for myself and be number one. As expected, Father Joseph was not pleased with my decision, but he understood. The public will not perceive the significance for me to walk away. I would like them to walk by my side for a month and then get their opinions.

One good thing is, Father Joseph will not have to look at my ugly mug almost every day. It is getting closer and closer for my final day on the job. My patience is running short. I am afraid that I will not be able to refrain myself from telling people to go fly a kite, say inappropriate comments that would hurt their feelings that might end up in an argument.

I cannot concentrate like I did in the past. To be able to guide spirits, you need to really focus or concentrate which is beginning to be a problem. I might make a mistake that could make it difficult or even prevent the spirit to reach the gates of heaven.

I will never forgive myself if I drop the ball, which resulted in a predicament that the spirit would have no choice but to go on his own and failed to get to heaven because of my blunders.

My family doctor told me I am suffering from mental fatigue, and I need to start taking care of myself as soon as possible, otherwise, it could completely ruin my health and go into a deep depression. As per my doctor, if I fall into the deep hole of depression, it is very hard, sometimes, impossible to climb the ladder to reach the surface.

Every day for as long as I can remember, I can feel a dark presence by my side. I do not know if the dark shadows, each take turns to accompany me or do shift work. If not, my comrade who is always with me must be dog tired.

My fellow citizens, quite a few actually, keep reminding me that I will never succeed in building a barrier between me and the spirits so that I can retire. I always utilize the same line: *'Can I take a look at your diploma? Because you seem to know more than I do when it comes to retirement. Have you done some research to back your words?'*.

"I would be surprised if you did, so you are not qualified to assume the way I will feel. Can you give me a prescription for retirement pills? Walk in my shoes for a couple of days and it would give you a small preview or an idea of what my life looks like."

They always look at me with no response to my questions.

"If you cannot do that, keep your ass sniffer out of my business and your comments right where your ass sniffer can get a good wiff, and get my drift. So, shove off, go try to resolve your own problems."

A certain comment that caught my ear is that: some people say that I am very courageous. For me, it is obvious because I am always in the public eye. Deep down inside, we are all courageous. We always find that extra gear when we need it. Even in the darkest hours, we push forward.

One of my dear friends that I do not get the chance to often to enjoy quality time with him and his family. I was thrilled when he broke the news that he was coming over with his family for a visit. The plan is-- they would stay for the weekend.

I assumed that he was aware there was a possibility that the house would be haunted. The two kids will sleep in what used to be my daughter's bedroom. His boys were eight and ten years of age. My friend and his wife will sleep in what used to be my son's room which we renovated and made a guest room

First thing when they arrived, they put their luggage in the bedrooms after a great dinner and a wonderful, pleasant evening, and a long enjoyable day for them. They drove four hours to get to my house. We were all fatigued and we retired for the night.

All through the house, no creature was stirring not even a mouse. Sorry wrong story. Everyone was sound asleep when the entities made their presence known to my guests. My friend's better half was awakened when the glass of water that was on the night table was poured in her face. My friend could feel a burning sensation on his toes. One of the boys was pushed out of bed.

I jumped out of bed to investigate what the heck was going on. My friend was in the hallway, furious because I did not warn them that the house was haunted.

"I am really, really, sorry. I assumed you knew."

"No, I did not have a clue. I know what you do but it never dawned on me that there would be ghosts in your house."

His wife was packing, the boys were crying.

"We are leaving."

"In the middle of the night? Come on now. We can talk about this in the morning."

"No, I do not care about talking in the morning. We are getting the hell out of here, so much for a nice weekend."

"I am truly sorry, but you should look in the mirror to see the expression on your face. It's priceless."

"Go ahead. Have fun at my expense."

"I apologize for having a smile on my face but it is funny."

His wife glanced at me.

"Maybe for you but not for us, some friend you are. I will never set foot in this house again."

She looked at my friend.

"Are you ready to go?"

"I was sure you knew that my house might be haunted."

"I did not and goodbye. You can count yourself lucky that we have been close friends for so many years because you would be the recipient of a knuckle sandwich right between the eyes."

Again, I reiterated,

"I swear, I was under the impression that you were aware. Let me make amends."

"It's not necessary. I have to go my wife and kids are waiting for me in the car."

"Will this event damage our friendship? I hope not."

He looked at me.

"We will see."

After my friend is gone, my wife was not happy with me.

"Why did you laugh? It was like putting salt in a gaping wound."

"I know, but I could not help it."

"They were all scared out of their minds. Poor kids, an event like that can scar them for life. They now know that ghost really exist. Do you think that it will affect your friendship?"

"To be honest, I do not know. I hope not."

I have not seen or talked to him since that evening.

For fun, I would make up stories. I could see the devil walking beside my friends when they were all hooked, worried, and jittery from my fibs. The anticipation that they might find themselves on the battlefield facing off against Satan, only to advise them not to be alarmed; it was all a fabrication, deceptions that I cooked up to have my fun at their expense.

When they tried to get even with me, I would fake going into a trance, so they would leave me alone. It was hilarious to see their reactions or facial expressions, precious moments that no money can buy. Good times that I will bring with me to my grave.

Throughout the book, I touched on reincarnation. I am a true believer. I guided the same spirit twice. Years ago, I guided the soul of an eighty-one-year-old woman. Recently, I guided the same soul to heaven.

The spirit of a twelve-year-old boy who drowned while swimming with friends. Souls have different flares of their own virtues, ethics. That is why, I can recollect having guided the same spirit a second time.

(Death is a window to another life; resurrection when we come back. Some of us to finish paying our karmic debt from previous lives. Our lives are transformed by the holy spirit.)

(The metaphorical "two edge sword" implies that the word of god drives a wedge between the elect and the reprobate, identifying the wicked and collecting the elect reinforcing the paradox that the body of believers is both inclusive and that one must go on living and striving.)

(Death is not always as safe as we think it is. The sad truth is that the devil wants each one of us dead, but thank god, Jesus offers us eternal life. Who hears his words and believe in him who sent everlasting life and shall not come into judgment but has passed from death to life. That is why, guidance to heaven is so important.)

(Reincarnation is the philosophical or religious concept that an aspect of a living being starts a new life in a different physical body or form after each biological death. It is also the rebirth or transmigration and in part of the samsara doctrine of cyclic existence.)

It all makes sense now when I say I am a recycled teenager or a middle-aged juvenile; yes indeed. My friends break out in laughter when I mention my famous phrases.

For some non-believers when they die, their body will be six feet under and nothing exist anymore that was part of them. Everything is buried with them. Souls, heaven, hell… for them does not exist. You decompose in your grave and that is the end of your existence. There is no coming back.

I beg to differ. When I am having a conversation with a family member in which I guided their loved one to heaven, I always feel the spirit by my side listening. When the conversation is over, the spirit goes back to heaven.

(Origin of reincarnation first recorded 1855-60. There is a notion of reincarnation namely that our children are really returning ancestors, being reborn in another body. Several religions, including Hinduism, believe that

the human spirit returns to earth in different forms again and again, and it strives for perfection.)

I have stated a few times that I truly believe that perfection does not exist. Nothing can be perfect, there are always modifications that can be made. For me, the word perfection is overrated. That's my personal view on the matter.

A majority of the population across the world say that reincarnation is a myth, but it does not stop people asking me questions like, *'I keep dreaming about my mom who died several years ago, does that mean that she is alive somewhere in the world?'*.

'If I die from a disease, will I reincarnate with the same illness?' I advise them to do their own research because I do not have the answers they are looking for.

When people say when they almost died, they saw members of their family that passed, they saw heaven, etc. Some critics say, it is the brain reacting to a near-death experience. As per the critics, no souls are involved. Boy, I could be opening a can of worms if I was to give my opinion on the subject. The phenomena of near-death will always ignite debates among religious groups.

In the minds of some people, they believe that an indigo child has something to do with reincarnation and we come back as adults. We are born babies like every human being on this planet. The only distinction is that, we are gifted with a sixth sense. You do not need to be born an indigo child to be given a special gift at birth. Take psychics for example, Nostradamus, Einstein, and many more in history and the present day are very gifted individuals.

If you have doubts, you can find all the information you need in books or on the web. If you have doubts about past events in your life that reincarnation or the paranormal might have been involved, go back into your vault of memories. Talk to relatives and you might find the answers you are looking for.

(Karmic or karma is a cumulative result of effects which is created by an individual's will and actions throughout many lives on earth. In other words, karma is the soul's tendency formed during the process of

reincarnation people may talk about bad karma; but it is we who are creating our own karma through the choices and actions we take by being aware of our tendencies and making deliberate efforts to make better decisions.)

(We can change our fate to put it in a modern way, karma is the imprint of memories from past lives that remain in each soul so if you know someone like me who is always plagued by bad luck. It is a good chance; they might be paying their karmic debt from previous lives.)

Before writing the book, I did some research on reincarnation and karmic debt. I must have been a real bad boy and done terrible things in my previous lives that I am plagued with bad luck.

Bad luck is now my middle name. I hope I will be able to pay my debt in full before I kick the bucket so that I can enjoy a less stressful and comfortable life on my next tour on Earth. Father Joseph emphasized that according to his chart, my karmic debt is paid in full.

A mistake was probably made on the chart, yes it subsided for a small period of time but it is back in full swing. I am conscious that the entities do bring some bad luck. I am convinced that the entities are not always guilty of making my life luckless. I am convinced that I still owe a few invoices on my karmic account.

A good percentage of the population is clueless, no knowledge that grasshoppers is a delicacy for the devil. If you notice an increase of grasshoppers on your lawn or anywhere else in your yard for that matter... Beware! Be on your toes. Watch for an entity.

The devil might be manifesting for no apparent reasons. He will invade your life and your house. My neighbor once caught site of the abundance of grasshoppers around my house and none on his property. My excuse was, *'You mow your lawn more often than I do'*. They love the tall grass.

"I notice when your done cutting your grass, I can still detect quite a few grasshoppers remaining on your lawn."

"I think they prefer the type of soil and seeds that I used for my lawn. Probably a buffet for them."

"Could be."

I do not know if he believed me or not. A couple of weeks later, we were having a chat when he turned the conversation into something that he might have seen in his garage. He was not sure, but he might have seen a phantom in his garage.

"If it is a ghost, I will show him who is the boss around here and make it scram from my garage."

"I hope it was not an entity that you saw. If it is, take safety measures, and never sell short the power of an evil entity. Never assume anything that might bite you in the ass, you never know what is on their mind."

A month passed when I inquired if he again spotted the ghost.

"No."

"Good for you."

In the old days, nobody was brave enough to come forward and report some paranormal activities. If they did, people would say that they were crazy or maybe they were practicing witchcraft.

If it could be proven, the lady was a witch, and her husband was a warlock. They were hung. Some generations believed in werewolves, vampires, and ghosts. That's probably the time in history when people were not afraid anymore to come forward to tell their stories.

The population was flooded with rumors, exaggerations, embellishments, stories that would make your head spin… you name it. Now, the devices that paranormal investigators now use, defy logic and proof of paranormal activity.

The critics are not sold. They come up with ludicrous explanations and theories that do not make any sense for instance nowadays; trail cameras take pictures of weird animals, ghosts, spirits, aliens, bigfoot, and other creatures that are out there.

They go about in silence. Aliens descend from the skies. Aliens' abductions. Dark spirits invade, and take control of a human host to survive. Once they have infected their victims, they can assume any deadly form they choose.

Monsters with giant teeth, winged demons, and creatures with long fingers for hands and most have chosen to conceal their lethal purpose bigfoots witnessed by so many people in my neck of the woods including myself.

After spending a weekend at my camp. I was driving home on the remote road that I always drive through to get to my camp. In the distance, I could see the sun fading. The sun was going to bed. I turned on my headlights.

I spotted a female bigfoot with her young one running across the road. I got out of the truck close to the spot where they ran in the bush; I grabbed my flashlight and ventured into the bush hoping to get another glimpse at the creatures to take a few pictures for proof they do exist.

The sun was going down, darkness was fast approaching. I did not want to take a chance to go any further and not be able to get back to the truck. I made my way back to the road upset that I was not able to spot anything.

They must have found a place to hide. I would not be surprised if they were looking straight at me. I kept the bigfoot sighting to myself. I did not want to deal with more controversy. Years ago, three of my friends went on a camping trip. They were supposed to be camping for three days. I was surprised and curious as to why they came home after only one day.

My friend filled me in on the details. Two of my friends were sleeping in the tent. He was extinguishing the campfire when he heard some noise coming from the bushes.

He grabbed his flashlight and went to investigate the source of the noise. It was a full moon from a distance he saw something large moving. He tiptoed a little closer to get a better look when he realized that he was witnessing a bigfoot eating berries.

He turned off his flashlight and tiptoed back to the camp. He was very careful not to make any noise and be spotted by the bigfoot. Back at the campsite, he woke up the two friends and advised them not to make any noise.

All three made their way to the truck without making a sound. They gently opened one door of the truck and made their way inside. Closed the door just enough to turn off the light in the cab.

They were too nervous to sleep, and afraid bigfoot would make its way to their campsite. In the morning, they gathered their stuff trying to be as quiet as possible. All three were anxious to get home.

My friends did not say a word to anyone except me about the sighting. They did not want to be ridiculed and argue with the public. Children who died, came back and disclose they talked to Jesus. Television series of lost tapes, angels caught on camera, shows of paranormal activities, books on exorcism, and hauntings.

People who died and doctors were able to resuscitate them, they have a story to tell. They were able to see family members who passed away, and also described what heaven looks like.

If you are constantly waking up or awake between three and four in the morning. We all know between three and four AM is the witching hour. It might be because spirits are trying to communicate with you or manifest for one reason or another.

Demons strive during the witching hour. I have written about the subject earlier in the book. Just a reminder of what you could expect when the clock strikes three am.

As a firefighter/first responder, I have witnessed things that no human should not be able to see. When I joined the fire department, I was educated by more than one confrere that, when battling a blaze, if you see a statue, picture, crucifix or anything that was blessed, it will not burn.

Might be damaged a little bit but will not burn. The flames will bypass the objects even if the house is burnt to the ground. You will find religious items in the rubble or a wall that is still standing. You can see where the flames bypassed the picture on the wall,

"You guys are pulling my leg."

"We are not pulling your leg, just wait and see. It is an amazing phenomenon to witness. You have to see it to believe it."

Over the years, I have witnessed it more than once. For me to see it for the first time, I was mesmerized. There are guardian angels with you all the time. They are pure beings of divine light which I have seen a number of times, whom we can trust, and they want to help in every aspect of our lives. Archangels are not human; they are celestial beings.

There are more archangels than people realize. The most popular are archangels Michael, Gabriel, and Raphael; all three have been mentioned in the bible.

Heavenly beings, much like angels, are forms that live amongst the heavens. Although not completely like a spirit, they take the form of humans and they have the power to conjure weapons called sacred weapons or jingi to aid them in battle. Like humans, heavenly beings are able to channel their internal power. Heavenly beings are able to walk on all three planes in paradise.

There are three heavens mentioned in the bible: the third one-- god's throne, the second heaven -- outer space, and first heaven-- earth's atmosphere.

Sometimes when you achieve the impossible, angels are helping you. Some are human angels, if someone or a stranger that you became friends with, without his or her help you would not have been able to achieve your goal. It is not by coincidence; he or she was waiting to meet you and help you.

Do not be discouraged by your incapacity to dispel darkness from the world. Light your candle and step forward. For certain things, sometimes, you need to be patient and never lose hope. I myself, came close a few times to losing hope. It is not a good feeling. No matter what you do or what the day brings, tomorrow will come anyway. We cannot alter the clock of life.

I wish we could. Tomorrow will come; a new day that has never been touched. Remember, dreams never die, just the dreamer. We are all born innocent, and we all die guilty of something.

Some spirits travel in dimensions through mirrors, strange pathways, or gateways. There are a lot of tormented and desperate souls trying to find the path to forgiveness. These souls knew that every action brings a reaction. While living, they did not care about reactions and look where they are now.

There is a universal, energetic field that flows through everyone and everything. We need to learn how to use that energy to keep going with our day-to-day life.

As the saying says, *'You do not know what you have until it is gone'*. Even if we cannot imagine how life will be when they are gone. All of us have lost loved ones. We all have different courses of action to cope with. Sometimes, we are surprised about how much we miss him or her once they are gone.

Chapter 21

This is the final chapter of the book. If I keep writing, the book would have no ending. I am mentally drained. I am at the end of my rope of hearing noise in the basement, cabinets, cupboards opening by themselves.

What I am describing right now is only the tip of the iceberg for all the events and manifestations taking place almost every day. My house is a real chatterbox for spirits. When looking outside and see the face of the devil in the window and faces on the TV screen.

There must be a ton of unhappy, depressed souls. I can hear constant sobbing almost every night. I wake up between three and four am. Bangs on the walls pictures flying across a room.

I rarely get a good night sleep without being harassed by bad spirits, entities, and so on. It is taking its toll on my health: high blood pressure, lack of sleep, and my patience is all but gone. I do not have the energy, the fighting spirit anymore. Father Joseph noticed, the fire in my eyes to get things done was diminishing at a rapid pace. So enough is enough before I lose what is left of my sanity.

I did more than my fair share. I have put a wall between me and everything that relates to spirits and the paranormal. I am aware, I will keep on dreaming and travel from one galaxy to another and other worlds. I know that some people still have questions, again demanding the impossible.

Lately, when I go into a trance, I end up with headaches. I cannot leave my body anymore and float with the spirit until it reaches the gates of heaven without consequences. I want to live a normal life for a change. I want to know how the other half lives.

I made reference a few times in the book that I would not give up. I am not giving up. I am retiring; no more slaps in the face while sleeping. I am ready to go forward with a new beginning. I have been judged, people made fun of me, yelled at shoved, called names. I was the recipient of bad jokes, dumb comments by individuals from every walk of life.

How you see your fellow man or woman can make a big difference in everyone's life; do not assume until you know the facts. I once confided in a friend that I was certain I could trust him. I got burned to aches in a matter of hours, on every street corner, people were yapping away about the big secret that I wanted to hide from the public.

It was not a secret. It was information from a variety of situations that were very difficult to deal with, that brought tears to my eyes. No matter what went down I never divulged any names.

Yes, I am walking away. It is time for me to retire and withdraw to my own little piece of paradise. The spirits/souls that I assisted for them to go upstairs into the big house, will always be with me. They are locked in my heart, and I threw away the key.

One of the deciding factors is-- constant bad luck. Like I said before, Father Joseph advised me that my karmic debt was paid. I think he made a mistake with my chart. I know bad luck will persist until my debt is paid.

If I retire, all the bad luck the entities were sending my way will come to an end. Father Joseph did warn me as long as I keep guiding spirits, the dark side will continue to provide me with unpleasant surprises. I was injured more than once-- broken ribs, scratches and bruises all over my body.

I was also plagued with spirits that sold their souls to satan, and kept harassing me for redemption. I turned them down some more than once by reminding them it was god that would decide their fate, not me.

Some were displeased with me due to my replies. They would come and cause some mischief in the house, knocking a lamp of a table, whistling in my ears etc... ghosts, spirits or similar entities would materialize in human form.

My biggest fear and worry was to let people down and lose their trust. Except for the time I went on that ridiculous drinking rampage. What brought me joy was the fact, people would come to me and say thank you and telling me I was right in my predictions, and they were now believers.

We are fools to believe that we are alone in the universe and life itself. We are surrounded by spirits. As I look back over the years, could I have done more? I guess I will never know, but one thing is for sure: I always did my best. One thing that I learned rather quickly is: To cast out demons, you must have authority on them. Show them who's the boss.

Many brilliant minds believed they did not possess genius but rather genius possessed them like a spirit. It does not matter who or what you are and what you do as long as you show kindness to your fellow beings, then they will be kind to you.

While I was in the process of writing the book, I would always hear annoying soft knocks on the wall. Even when I switched rooms in the house so I could write in peace and quiet, no such luck. I would still hear the annoying knocks on the wall.

Whoever or whatever was given the task of doing the knocking, I have to admit he was doing a good job. Kudos to him or her. He was very persistent, never missed a beat. His/her superiors should give him/her an award for a job well done. As soon as I opened my laptop like clockwork, I could hear knocking on the wall.

When finalizing my book I mentioned that I would block everything to do with spirits, but I am afraid some souls will always fall between the cracks. I was on my way home, someone came to mind.

I was puzzled as to why the gentleman was in my brain that day. The following day, I learned that the man passed away the day before.

I knew who he was but did not know him personally. Will I ever be able to escape?

I am aware there are still a big number of non-believers out there. Some have not yet witnessed an event to convince them to change their minds, some refuse to believe, to each our own.

Until that fateful night. I was a rebel, dismissing facts as fast as a man with the runs looking for a toilet. I used to shoot off my big mouth. Nothing would convince me to change my way of thinking when it comes to the paranormal. Boy, I was proven wrong!

A bad habit that we humans have is we assume to quickly judge and criticize before digging for the truth. There is always a reason, either good or bad, for our actions. One phrase that I kept repeating, *'I did not request to be born an indigo child'*. I did not have a chance to choose the cards that were dealt for me.

Once the deck of cards is shuffled and the cards are on the table, it is what it is. We need to accept our role in society. I am no different than anybody else on this earth. We are brought into this world without having the chance to choose where, when, or why we are born.

My kids endured a lot of taunting from other kids. Basically, almost everywhere they went. A smartass kid would start teasing which resulted in a chain reaction; every kid would get in on the action. I would always preach to the pesky brats, 'If you have to hurt other people in order to feel powerful, you are an extremely weak individual'.

My son took boxing lessons, and he is also left-handed. Quite frankly, he was very good at boxing. He started to kick ass. The bully boys finally retreated and mind their own business. The same for my daughter, she also took boxing lessons. She was also able to take care of herself.

My tasks where not like a 9 to 5 job. Close the shop for the day and go home. My personal life was affected more ways than one. I was married to the mother of my children, and we eventually divorced. Afterwards, I was engaged to a wonderful woman. The marriage never took place.

We ended up going our separate ways. I was involved in another relationship that went down the tubes. I finally met and married the woman of my dreams, we are still going strong. No cracks in our foundation.

My obligations prevented me from accomplishing things that I wanted to do-- follow my dreams. Some citizens still believe that I am living in a make believe world. It is all a fantasy. Yeah right, some fantasy. I am not guilty of certain things that the population accused me of like exploiting from the public or I was able to feast on the vulnerable. Contrary to belief, I am not on drugs.

Like I said, people really fascinate me. Stupid things some people do and what comes out of their mouths. We could have a twenty-four-hour party of laughter and be in the book of Guinness World Records. One thing is for certain, there would be an abundance of events, situations and conversations that would result in non-controllable laughter.

We all have a purpose in life, a reason to be here. If you already know what your purpose in life is, that's great. The ones that do not know yet, one day you will realize what is your purpose. The reason why you are walking on this earth and the crazy world we live in. No matter how big or small, you will be able to say, *'I made a difference today'*.

Like I previously mentioned, every day we try to do our best. We do what we can, when we can with what we have. What lies for us on the horizon, we do not know. It is up to us to push forward full steam ahead to take on whatever the future holds for us.

If you decide that you're going to do only the things you know are going to work, you're going to leave a lot of opportunities on the table. Sometimes, you need to get out of your comfort zone and explore new options.

A lot of citizens inquired if I needed to leave my comfort zone to accomplish certain tasks... I did not have a comfort zone. For me, a new day was always a day of uncertainty about what the day might bring. Every day was a challenge. Do not forget that our time and resources are limited on earth, but our minds are limitless. Be kind to each other and God bless.

The End.